Isley

Pl

Lean
Skin A Cat
albatross
The Swell

With an introduction by Isley Lynn

methuen | drama

LONDON • NEW YORK • OXFORD • NEW DELHI • SYDNEY

METHUEN DRAMA
Bloomsbury Publishing Plc
50 Bedford Square, London, WC1B 3DP, UK
1385 Broadway, New York, NY 10018, USA
29 Earlsfort Terrace, Dublin 2, Ireland

BLOOMSBURY, METHUEN DRAMA and the Methuen Drama logo are trademarks
of Bloomsbury Publishing Plc

First published in Great Britain 2024

A catalogue record for this book is available from the British Library.

A catalog record for this book is available from the Library of Congress.

ISBN: PB: 978-1-3505-0452-3
        ePDF: 978-1-3505-0453-0
        eBook: 978-1-3505-0454-7

Series: Contemporary Dramatists

Typeset by RefineCatch Limited, Bungay, Suffolk
Printed and bound in Great Britain

Contents

Introduction

by Isley Lynn

To publish a Plays One has been a dream of mine ever since I decided to become a playwright. I imagined it would signify having made it as a proper grown-up playwright. That this dream is coming true within a year of winning an award for 'Most Promising Playwright' is an irony not lost on me. It's an almost too-perfect illustration of how nonlinear this industry is, and how serpentine the paths through it can be. I have peers who seem to be able to get on a career ladder and simply climb it rung by rung, but that's certainly not been my experience. I'm very aware that my career is as much down to my tenacity as my talent. This is often a source of a lot of pain. But I'm also proud of it.

When people ask me why I became a playwright, I like to glibly tell them that it's because I'm lazy: I hate learning new skills, and the government forced me to learn how to spell and hold a pen. Plus novels are too long, and only half of a play happens on the page – the rest is achieved by other people.

The truth is that while I'd always written from a young age – in the way which is true of many people (dream-fulfilment fiction and bad poetry) – I just never stopped. I went to Exeter University thinking I'd be a director, but I realised that I didn't just want to tell stories, I wanted to have a say in what stories got told; the plays I was reading seemed to all regurgitate the same old plots with the same old characters, and didn't reflect the world that I was living in or the people I loved that populated it. Spending hours slogging through boring plays with piss-poor representation galvanised me to commit to only writing what I thought contributed something I knew to have truth, and was new to what already exists.

But the *real* truth is I was doomed to be a playwright. I don't love anything else as much. I'm not as good at anything else. There's nothing else that enters my mind unbidden. During the bleakest parts of the pandemic, I considered the potential death of live art forms, and gave serious thought to what else I could do for money. But I would always slide into dreaming up a play set in the imagined territory of that fantasy career. I consider this tunnel vision a blessing. I have so many multi-talented friends who can become paralysed in deciding what to pursue, or stretched thin between their various passions. What a relief to only be good at one thing.

So I was always going to write plays, whether any potential employers paid attention or not. For me, writing is a way of being in the world, of processing my experiences, of externalising parts of myself to see them better, or to dive deeply into other people and understand them. My partner (who this collection is dedicated to) is a painter, and we share this compulsion to figure out ourselves by figuring out someone else. It's his work that graces the front cover – a portrait-in-progress which retains the marks of this figuring, and for me represents the endeavour to capture someone's humanity, which is at the heart of everything I write too.[1]

I'm lucky that my family is littered with arts lovers, and my mother's first career as an opera singer meant that a career in the arts wasn't a silly pipe dream, but something I had witnessed from a young age. My parents have always been extraordinarily supportive – when my Year 7 English teacher told them that I had talent to take seriously, they asked him not what careers it might be useful for, but simply what they should do to nurture it. He told them to take me to as many plays as possible. And they did. I remember feeling rocked with incredulity that I was sharing air with my first celebrity crush Alan Rickman when they took me to see him and Lindsay Duncan in *Private Lives* at the then-Albery Theatre. It was the same fizz I felt watching my mother onstage, and recognising her secret wave to us as we watched her from up in the nosebleed section.

That unwavering support and encouragement equipped me with a confidence bordering on entitlement that has seen me through the turbulence of being chronically freelance. But it also meant that I was in for a shock when I graduated and entered an industry heaving with talented writers – being good at dialogue and a pleasure to have in class wasn't going to cut it anymore. I've always thrown myself into things I care about, but developing a proper work ethic was the first test of my professional life. And while my expectation was that all the new writing venues would fight over my debut play, the reality was that every production I've had has been a fight for its existence. The plays in this collection were all scrappy, and they all have tales of trials behind them:

Lean was my first ever play, which started as a writing assignment for my playwriting module at uni. We were tasked with writing an outline and the first twenty minutes of a full-length play. My lecturer's feedback was lukewarm, but I was excited about the idea and keen to finish it. I sent it to everyone, and received encouraging responses (letters in those days), but it was Ben Monks at the Tristan Bates Theatre (which had an open script submission policy, despite not being a producing theatre) who asked for a meeting and said to get in touch if I ever got a producer behind it. It was developed through Angelic Tales at the Theatre Royal Stratford East, and

---

1   It also represents a transience that theatre shares – this portrait was destroyed in a moment of self-doubt, and all that remained were two very damaged slides bearing a photograph he'd taken partway through the process of painting it. We had the image restored from those slides.

an actor in that reading shared it with a director she knew, who shared it with a producer she was in touch with, and when everyone was set to do it, I got back in touch with Ben. He was true to his word and he and Will Young, his Co-Creative Producer, programmed it for the start of 2013. There was no money in it for anyone, and my partner built the highly naturalistic set in the sixty-seater studio using the discarded remnants of the producer's day job boss's newly-renovated kitchen.

Skin A Cat got me a lot of attention, but I struggled to find it a home at first. Everyone seemed to love it, but many found the content 'too niche'; I scratched the first scene of the show to a 'feedback audience' and everyone cackled so loudly that the actors had to keep pausing and we overran. But one guy told me off for writing something that half the audience (the men) couldn't relate to. His play was about a man going to Mars. . . Others wanted to change the fundamentals of the play's form, to make it easier to stage. The director of its reading as part of IdeasTap's Takeover Festival said to me: 'Sex on stage is tricky, can all these sex scenes be just talked about afterwards?' Another suggested I distill the story down to a relationship drama between just a few characters. So when Blythe Stewart understood what the play was and why that was important, I practically threw it at her; she applied to VAULT Festival 2016, we got accepted, our producer dropped out, we put it on with no money and the designer's own bra in the costume, we sold out our week run and won Pick Of The Year, which led to us being the inaugural show at the Bunker Theatre.[2]

Albatross was a student show commissioned by Paines Plough and the Royal Welsh College of Music and Drama for their groundbreaking NEW Festival. I received a bit of pressure to write a story with a protagonist and a swirling multitude of characters around them, partly because I'd done that successfully in *Skin A Cat*, but also because of how Paines Plough programmed their Roundabout space at the time: a company of three actors in rep across multiple plays, which mine could be considered for after the student shows. But to do that would serve one student much more than the others. It just didn't sit well with me, and I stood firm, instead writing a play where the role of protagonist ricochets around the cast of characters, which I've had the joy of seeing performed by many student groups since.

The Swell was the first idea I ever had for an original play. It almost received a production plenty of times over the course of many years, but gatekeepers always wanted to make it smaller or cheaper or attach people

---

2 IdeasTap, VAULT Festival, and The Bunker Theatre have all since disappeared and, as someone who relied on them to cut my teeth when I wasn't finding opportunities to stage my work through established companies or venues, a theatre landscape without these crucibles of creativity looks incredibly bleak.

with bigger names to it. I turned down a few chances to get it on because all of those offers came with terms which would fundamentally diminish the play in some way. It was always a devastating decision to make, and I feared the play would end up relegated to the dreaded drawer. That it has now received praise and accolades is a massive validation of my obstinance, and proof that so often the reason your work isn't getting the support it deserves is nothing to do with the work itself. The script remained stubbornly unchanged from when I first sent it out to its premier at the Orange Tree Theatre, so it's not that it needed that time to develop into something stage-worthy. It needed someone like Tom Littler and the team to programme it without demanding a compromise of vision.

I share these stories because I wish I'd heard more of them when I was starting out. I remember trying to pry them from a playwright alumni who came back for a Q&A, but they only shared the string of hotshots who all simply loved their plays and put them on, just like that. I've been carving out a playwriting career for well over a decade and I still benefit so much from hearing how others get the work not just written, but made. So much of my career is still driven by my own hustle. Until recently I've earned money by life modelling and running workshops for arts charities and baking carrot cakes for posh delicatessens, and I'm thrilled to have never had to ask my parents for money to stay afloat, but the security of their safety net allowed me to take risks that kept my career progressing when I wasn't making money from it.

But there's another risk to doing something with an unreliable source of income, especially if it's something you love: What if you doggedly pursue it and you never make a living from it? What if that critically-acclaimed play was just a flash in the pan? What if that dream is only ever something you did, once or twice, and it never becomes something you are? I live in fear that every production is the last production, and I think I always will, because so much of a writing career is out of the writer's control. Reminding myself of that sometimes makes me feel better, but most of the time it makes me feel worse. It's brutalising to know that the arts aren't a meritocracy, and that how great you are is only a small part of the puzzle. But knowing so does give you a gift of sorts: the freedom to devote your energy to the work, which is the only thing truly in your control. Making sure the work represents you, that you'd be happy for it to outlive you, even if no one ever sees it. And if the only thing you can control is the work, then the only thing you can always do is keep making the work, and hope that the world catches up. To simply keep going.

I kept going. And now I'm writing an introduction to my Plays One. Proof that I really did it, to some merit, and not just once. Now I've just got to keep going until Plays Two.

Lean

for Andrew, of course

Author's Note

When writing a new play, I always ask myself the following questions:

- Is the story, in some way, true?
- Is the story, in some way, useful?
- Do I have, or can I get, unique access to the subject matter, and in turn give an audience a unique perspective on the territory of the story?
- Does the story uniquely contribute to the stories that already exist?

The last two are perhaps the most pertinent to this play in particular. When I started writing *Lean*, I was in my final year of university and in a long-distance relationship with a 'recovering anorexic'. He subscribed to the idea that people with eating disorders are also addicts: never 'cured', always 'in recovery'. And he had started taking real steps to address his disordered eating around the same time as we started dating, so during the course of our relationship I saw his body and his personality transform.

What he told me about his relationship with food, and with not eating, was nothing like what I'd understood about anorexia before. I thought it would be useful, unique, and true to write a play that shared his experiences. And I had unique access in a boyfriend who was keen for me to write a character like him, and generous with his candour.

I'm proud that this is my first play to be staged, and to have done so with the very important charity Men Get Eating Disorders Too.

Thanks

Thanks to Rikki Beadle-Blair and John Russell Gordon, Chris Edgerley, John Foster, Laura Hanna, Bruce and Lori Lynn, Caroline Milsom and Jamie Rio, Ben Monks and Will Young, Grace Plant and Edward Plant, John Rook, Geoffrey Stuart, the Theatre Royal Stratford East, Chelsea Walker, Hilary Williamson, and all the original readers in Exeter 2009.

Lean premiered at the Tristan Bates Theatre in London on 29 January 2013. The cast was as follows:

Michael   Tim Dorsett
Tessa   Laura Hanna

Creative Team
Director   Chelsea Walker
Producer   Zoe Anjulia Robinson
Designer   Holly Pigott
Lighting Designer   Neill Brinkworth
Sound Designer   Robert Donnelly-Jackson
Movement Director   Sinéad O'Keeffe
Stage Manager   Colleen Jeffery
Asst. Stage Manager   Harriet Smith
PR   Kim Morgan
Set Construction   Geoffrey Stuart

Lean had a subsequent run at the Corpus Playroom in Cambridge, opening on 20 January 2015. The cast was as follows:

Michael   Gabriel Cagan
Tessa   Rose Reade

Creative Team
Director   Robbie Taylor Hunt
Associate Director   Laura Waldren
Assistant Director   Bea Svistunenko
Producer   Gabriel Agranoff
Stage Manager   Ted Loveday
Publicity Designer   Atri Banerjee
Master Carpenter   Lydia Clark, Jack Swanborough
Assistant Producer   Ellie Mitchell
Lighting Op   Evangeline Tsui, Isa Bonachera
Op Trainer   Johannes Ruckstuhl
Rigger   Jamie Fenton
Fridge Saviour   Tom Stuchfield
Photographer   Johannes Hjort

Lean then had the following runs:
6–8 April 2015 at Hackney Attic in London; 20–4 April 2018 at Wingate and Ring Theatres in North Carolina, USA; 22–30 May 2015 at N15 Theatre in London.

Key

If a character's line ends with— and their next lines begins with — then
the lines run on as one without pause
/ marks a point of interruption
Interrupted lines are still spoken in their entirety
[ ] indicates speech which is not said out loud but is included to clarify
the intention of the line

A kitchen. Fairly plain, not new-looking. Counter-tops line the back wall or stand as an isolated island. There is the usual collection of appliances, including specifically a microwave, a telephone, a small television, a sink and a fridge. There is also a small table with two matching chairs. Above this hangs a lamp, lighting the space.

It is night. As the audience take their seats Michael sits at the table, working on a Sudoku puzzle.

Scene 1

Tessa *is at the kitchen door, carrying a bag, in a coat and gloves, which she takes off and puts in her pockets on seeing* **Michael**.

Tessa   I'm not coming back to you.

Michael   Ok.

Beat.

Tessa *puts her stuff down, keeping her coat on.*

Tessa   I'm back in the house, I'm not back with you.

Michael   Yes.

Beat.

What have you / come back for?

Tessa   She was right. You look / . . .

Michael   What?

Tessa   Said you were looking / . . .

Michael   Who?

Tessa   Your mother. She called me.

Michael   And you answered?

Beat.

Tessa   Give me your wallet.

Michael   What?

Tessa   Give me your wallet.

Michael   Why do you want my / wallet?

Tessa   Just give it to me, Michael.

Michael   What for?

Tessa   Give it to me!

Michael   Tess just tell me.

Tessa   I swear to god if you don't / . . . [give me that fucking wallet]

Michael *gets out his wallet and tosses it on the table towards her.* **Tessa** *shuts up. She then picks up the wallet and rapidly pulls out the receipts, looking through each one.*

Michael   What are you doing?

Tessa *doesn't respond.*

Michael   What are you / . . . [doing]

Tessa   None from the supermarket! You haven't been buying food, Michael.

Pause.

Tessa *frantically starts looking in all the cupboards.*

Tessa   There's no food in the house.
(*turning to him*) Where's the food?

Silence.

Tessa *sits down.*

Tessa   You're an idiot.

Michael   Don't call me an idiot, Tess.

Tessa   Stop being so stupid and I will!

Michael   Listen, I know you're upset / . . .

Tessa   This isn't my fucking period! I'm pissed off! At you!

Silence.

So what do I do? Take you to the clinic? Call up Brown? 'Sorry, Doc, I left him alone for two seconds and he's fallen off the wagon . . .'

Michael   I didn't want you to know. I didn't want my mother to know . . .

Tessa   Well your mother is smarter than you. It's all I can do, isn't it. I'm moving back in. Until you're better. Then I'll go.

Michael   You aren't serious.

Tessa   I'm not joking.

Michael   You're moving back in?

Tessa   Yes.

Michael   For how long?

Tessa   That depends on you, doesn't it.

Michael   What about work?

Tessa   I took sabbatical.

Michael   You should be on holiday.

Tessa   Well I'm here.

Michael   Where are you going to sleep?

Tessa   You're not putting up much of a fuss / about my coming back . . .

Michael   Of course not. Why / would I?

Tessa   Nobody wants you slipping back into old habits.

Michael   It's not a habit.

Tessa   Whatever it is I'm not going through all this shit again, we've done all that shit. All the psychiatrists and-and dieticians and counselors and Bonny fucking Brown! And it didn't work! Why do it again? I'm not going to do it again. You hear me?

Beat.

I'm going to live here. With you. And I'm not going to leave. And if you won't eat, then I won't either. I won't let a single bite pass my lips until it passes yours and I'll show you what you're doing to yourself. And if you won't get healthy to save *yourself*, then . . .

Tessa *waits for a response, but* **Michael** *isn't looking at her.*

Tessa   Well?

No response from **Michael**.

Tessa   Say something, Michael.

Michael   This has all happened, very fast. Give me a – [second] I need to – [think]

Beat.

This isn't easy. You know it's not. You can't do it.

Tessa   Where do you get off telling me what I can and can't do?

Michael (*breaking*)   Where do you get off! Barging back in here after a year of silence! Not 'two seconds', a whole year of total silence, Tess!

Tessa   Just do what I tell you. Please. Don't make this any more difficult. You should be happy now, I'm back.
I'm back with you.

Michael   I didn't bring you back here, I / didn't ask for you back.

Tessa   No, I seem to remember you begging.

Michael   For you, us, not the hollow / body of . . . [my wife]

Tessa   Hollow! I'm not hollow, Michael! I'm full up with this fucking –! I had left you! I got away, salvaged my life and escaped you, and I wasn't well again, I wasn't over it, I will never get over it, Michael, but I was getting so much better and so much stronger and all it takes is one phone call to bring me all the way back here! With you! And I never thought, never wanted to do this, be here again.

Silence.

Get your stuff. You'll sleep on the sofa.

Scene 2

Tessa *and* **Michael** *sit opposite each other at the kitchen table. It is the next morning, and* **Tessa** *is wearing a jumper and trousers,* **Michael** *wears the same trousers as before with an old t-shirt that he has slept in.*

Michael   . . . Sleep well?

Tessa   I'm not doing that.

Michael   Sleep?

Tessa   Pleasantries. I'm doing something very specific.

Michael   Fine.

Tessa   And I'm not interested / in . . .

Michael   Fine!

Beat.

You should know. I've had a significant head start.

Tessa   How long of a head start?

Michael   A couple of weeks.

Tessa   A couple?

Michael   Three.

Tessa   That's not long.

Michael   It doesn't take long.

Tessa   I need to know your habits.

Michael   I told you it's not a / habit.

Tessa   Habit, I know. But your routine, do you start each day with, I don't know, an allowance? Or a game plan? Do you have any strategies at all?

Michael   You've seen me. I just – don't – eat.

Tessa   I need to know what I'm in for.

Michael   Not much.

Tessa   What about drinks?

Michael   I have coffee in the mornings. It takes away the oily taste in my mouth.

Tessa   Tea?

Michael   No.

Tessa   What about juice?

Michael   It's normally too rich, but sometimes.

Tessa   Milk?

Michael   Definitely too rich.

Tessa   Well I don't like my coffee black like you.

Michael   Fine by me. Your rules.

Tessa   You're not even going to try and make a difference?

Michael   It's easier said than done.

Tessa   I cured you once. I'll do it again.

Michael   No one's asking you to.

Tessa   Yes you are. You've got my attention and now I'm here.

Michael   I'm not taking any responsibility for this, Tessa. You need my guilt for this to work, so I'm cutting that out now. In fact, maybe I'll make it worse.

Tessa   Oh really?

Michael   Cold turkey.

Tessa   Or not, as the case may be.

Michael   I'm a pro. You're not, you'll buckle. I don't want to hurt you.

Tessa   Then eat something!

Michael   No!

Tessa   You're wrong. I'm not leaving.

Michael (*beat*)   Sometimes I drink sugar water. To keep me going. You can do that. If you want.

Tessa   Let me know when you make some.

Scene 3

Michael *is sitting at the table, watching* **Tessa** *opposite him as she raps her fingernails on the table, traces the marks in the wood with her fingers etc. She looks at* **Michael**.

Tessa   This is dull.

Michael *nods.*

Tessa   Already.

Beat.

I should keep a journal. Dear Diary – Day One: Fuck all. The house is the same, a bit dirtier. Michael's the same, a bit uglier . . .

Michael   I'm going to start ignoring you if you're just going to snipe at me all day.

Tessa   You can't ignore me.

Michael *doesn't respond.*

Tessa   Haha.

Michael *doesn't respond.* **Tessa** *now matches him with her own silence. They stare at each other.*

Michael, *knowingly, picks up her Sudoku and begins a puzzle.* **Tessa** *makes many attempts to distract him, all to little avail.*

Michael   I suggest you get used to it. The boredom. You forget how much of the day is spent preparing and eating food. But you notice little things more.

Beat.

I used to get it into my head that all that time was wasted on food, that people were numbly following along, wasting their day. And I didn't need to. I was living, really living. If I stopped feeding my body I could feed my mind! I didn't need food. I was super human.

Tessa   You were an idiot.

Michael *strides to the kitchen counter and turns on the little TV. He props himself up and watches it.*

Tessa   What did you do? To get fired?

Michael   I didn't. I left.

Tessa   [But] You love the department?

Michael   Didn't seem important anymore.

Tessa   I don't know how you get through the day without a job. And this! It's just / so . . .

Michael   Meditative.

Tessa   No.

Michael   You don't think so?

Tessa   You can't meditate in front of a television. It doesn't count. It's cheating.

Michael   I'm not really watching. Besides, you've had more coffee than me. That's cheating. When was the last time you ate?

Tessa   I had dinner before I came.

Michael   Muslims do longer than that at Ramadan.

Tessa *gets up and turns off the TV.*

Tessa   I'll try harder. Reminds me though, I might call up Ameera while I'm here, she's the only person I really miss.

Michael   Thank you.

Tessa   It's the truth.

Michael   I'm aware.

Tessa   Why are you so passive aggressive?

Michael   Why are you so plainly aggressive!

Tessa   It's easy. You're weak, you even *look* weak. Your skin's flaking off . . .!

Michael   You fell in love with me like this.

Tessa   We were students, you wore it better then. Now you're older you just look dead. And there's something about seeing you like this, all pale and sickly . . .

Michael   Their daughter, she started big school this year.

Tessa   Really.

Beat.

Michael   You should call them, they ask after you. They've been bringing me food, even during the fasts. I couldn't turn it down. So I threw it out in little sections so they wouldn't notice.

Tessa   They were over?

Michael   Not a lot, but sometimes.

Tessa   They don't know, do they?

Michael   No. I never saw them at mealtimes – afternoons, late night movies . . .

Tessa   Well it looks like they didn't miss my company much . . .

Michael   What were they supposed to do, visit you at your brother's house?

Tessa   They could have! He likes guests, just not *you* showing up!

Micheal *moves over to the phone and picks it up, dialing.*

Michael   Call them, they'd love to / hear from you . . .

Tessa *darts over to* **Michael** *and slams the phone, still in his hand, down on the cradle. She keeps him pinned there.*

Tessa *releases* **Michael** *and storms to the TV, turns it on, and sits down at the table, focused on it, avoiding* **Michael's** *gaze.* **Michael** *watches her do all this and stays still for a moment before sitting himself down on the counter, watching the TV as well. They are silent as the screen flickers and screams.*

After a while:

Michael   You're procrastinating.

Tessa   Am I.

Michael   How long are we going to go without talking about it?

Tessa   *You* want to talk about it?

Michael   We have to.

Tessa   No we don't. Aren't you afraid of what I'll say?

Michael   You're not a complete bitch.

Tessa   I can be.

Michael   Yes.

They stare at the television.

Scene 4

It is that night, and **Tessa** *lies asleep at the table.* **Michael** *is also asleep, head against the cabinets and mouth wide open. The television is still on.*

A particularly loud commercial comes on and wakes **Michael***, who is startled but doesn't make much noise. He turns off the TV.*

He quietly moves to where **Tessa** *sleeps, about to wake her up. He stops himself and looks at her for a while. He permits himself to stroke her hair very gently, so as not to wake her.*

He takes the seat opposite her and watches her some more. He reaches across the table to lay his hand in hers. He settles down to sleep again.

This makes **Tessa** *open her eyes. She slowly looks over at him without moving. She looks at their hands. After a moment she calmly but briskly gets up and leaves the room without looking behind her, walking upstairs.* **Michael** *up watches her leave.*

Scene 5

Michael *is sitting at the kitchen table, working on another Sudoku puzzle.*

Tessa *is at the doorway, dressed in warm clothes with bags of groceries in her fists. She puts the food away as she talks.*

Michael   You went shopping?

Tessa   Must have done, mustn't I.

Michael   Kept the receipt?

Tessa   This is going to work. You'll be chubby in no time.

She lays ingredients on the counter and starts to take out utensils. She gets out a chopping knife and keeps it in her hand while she looks for a chopping board, but cannot find it. She turns to face **Michael**, *knife raised.*

Tessa   You've moved the chopping boards.

Michael   Ok. Put that down.

Tessa   Very funny where are they.

Michael   I moved them.

Tessa   I just said that.

Michael   They're in the side cupboard.

Tessa   Why did you move them?

Michael   I don't use them.

Tessa   You don't use anything because you don't eat.

Michael   I did eat, at first.

Tessa   But you didn't use chopping boards?

Michael   Mostly noodles.

Tessa   You can't live on noodles, Michael.

Michael   Yes, I figured that out fairly swiftly. So I / . . .

Tessa   Stopped eating altogether.

Michael   Switched to take-out.

Tessa   Michael . . .

Michael   At least that had some vegetables.

Tessa   What vegetables!

Michael   Well, like egg fried rice.

Tessa *stares at him blankly.*

Michael   It's got peas in it.

Tessa *laughs.*

Tessa   You're completely useless without me.

Michael *does not respond. Another awkward silence.*

Tessa   Side cupboard, did you say?

Scene 6.a

Tessa *and* **Michael** *are sitting opposite each other at the table. Cutlery and a steaming hot plate of lasagne sits in front of each of them.*

They stare at each other.

After a moment **Michael** *sighs and picks up his fork.* **Tessa** *picks up hers.*

He prods his food, leaning his head on his other hand. **Tessa** *watches him.*

Michael *looks at* **Tessa**, *she meets his eye. He deliberately and slowly places his fork back on the table.*

Tessa *keeps staring at him. She then places her fork down in a similar fashion.*

She picks up the plates and brings them to the bin, where she scrapes all the food into it.

Scene 6.b

Tessa *and* **Michael** *are sitting again at opposite ends of the table, with another meal in front of them – a fragrant curry. The television is on with commercials playing.*

Tessa *and* **Michael** *stare at each other.*

Tessa *takes the plates and scrapes the food into the bin.*

Scene 6.c

Tessa *and* **Michael** *are sitting again at opposite ends of the table, with another meal in front of them – a salad.*

Michael *and* **Tessa** *pick up their forks in perfect synchronization. They bring them up to the side of their heads, pointed upwards. They then both slowly put their forks back down.*

Tessa *takes the plates and scrapes the food into the bin.*

Scene 6.d

Tessa *and* **Michael** *are sitting again at opposite ends of the table, with another meal in front of them – rice and chicken.*

Michael *picks up his fork suddenly, and shovels a big forkful of food up from the plate.* **Tessa** *watches in awe.* **Michael** *dramatically brings the fork to his wide open mouth and pauses, looking out of the corner of his eye at* **Tessa**.

Michael   Ah!

Michael *and* **Tessa** *laugh jokingly as he puts the fork back down on the plate.*

Tessa *snatches the plates playfully and scrapes the food into the bin.*

Scene 6.e

Tessa *and* **Michael** *are sitting again at opposite ends of the table. A bowl of soup sits in front of each of them.*

They both play with their food, exhausted.

Tessa *stomps out of the room.* **Michael** *watches her go.*

Scene 7

Michael *is at the kitchen door – it is early morning, but* **Tessa** *is already in the kitchen: she has moved a kitchen chair to face the counter, looking*

out the window, and leans back on it, her legs propped up on the counter.
She is wearing a large fur coat and smoking a cigarette. A light sits on
the kitchen table, along with a few cigarette stubs.

Michael *starts at the sight of it, bemused.*

Michael   What are you doing?

Tessa *exhales in his direction.*

Michael   When did you start that again?

Tessa   This morning.

(referring to the coat) Remember this?

(tapping the pocket) I found them in here. Some are broken but still
good. I got the lighter from the drawer. And I started smoking at 4.45am.

Michael   I would be a hypocrite if I said you were killing yourself.

Tessa   Yeah you would be. Might as well go whole hog, I say.

Michael *sighs. He moves around a little, fidgety.* **Tessa** *remains calm,*
sipping slowly on her cigarette.

Michael *pauses, looking at the pack. He sits down at the table and picks*
it up. He carefully takes out a cigarette and spins it over in his fingers.
Tessa *has turned to watch him, mildly surprised.*

Michael *presents the cigarette to her, then places it between his lips.*
Tessa nods and smiles. **Michael** *smiles back, cocking his head a little,*
and lights it.

He inhales. There is a pause as the smoke swills around his lungs. His
eyes water. He coughs and sputters the smoke out, hacking and buckling
over. **Tessa** *laughs.*

Michael   I'll get the hang of it.

Tessa *(teasing)*   You're going to start?

Michael   You are.

Tessa   But I'm a smoker.

Michael   And I'm an anorexic.

Michael *takes another drag, with more success this time, but still*
uncomfortably.

Michael   Whole hog.

Tessa *shrugs. They both smoke.*

Michael   I couldn't get you to quit before. It was Jack who did that.

Silence.

They smoke.

Michael   Of course, this is cheating.

Tessa   Excuse me?

Michael *takes another drag.*

Michael   Hunger suppressant.

Michael, *coolly, powerfully, blows out his mouthful of smoke.* **Tessa** *gives him a burning look. She angrily stubs out her cigarette.*

Scene 8

Tessa *and* **Michael** *sit at the kitchen table, watching TV. A few more plates of food are sitting on the countertops. The Countdown music is playing and the microwave is on.*

Tessa   I've got 298.

Michael   Shh.

Tessa   But I've got the 7 left over . . .

Michael   In your head!

The music finishes and the players can be heard solving the problem. As they do this the microwave beeps and stops. **Tessa** *gets up and walks to it, taking out a small pizza and setting it on the table.*

As she sits back down she turns the television off with the remote and turns to **Michael**.

Michael   What did you do that for?

Tessa   [don't worry] I paused it.

Michael   I had it.

Tessa   I've figured it out. You're better at distracting yourself than I am. That's why I'm going round the twist while you just smile serenely. The television is definitely a distraction from food.

Michael   Or from you.

Tessa   Either way it's distracting.

Michael   You're right, of course it is, it's for distraction. And you were right when you said it was boring, it is. Fucking boring.

Beat.

It's good though, I can really *discover* silence if I try, which you can hardly ever / get in the real world . . .

Tessa   You're doing it again.

Michael   What?

Tessa   Distracting.

Michael   No I'm not.

Tessa   Yes you are. Rambling on esoterically is just as bad. Worse.

Michael   Alright.

Pause.

Michael *begins to pick at his fingernails with his fork.*

Tessa   Stop that!

Michael   What?

Tessa   Just put your hands on the table, palms down, and look at the pizza!

Michael *does so.*

Michael   Happy?

Tessa   Yes.

Michael   You know you'll just end up throwing it away and sulking –

Tessa   I don't sulk.

Michael   – because you're not winning.

Tessa   Not yet. But it's not too bad today, I don't like pepperoni.

Michael   Smart move. I wish you'd stop wasting the money frankly. Or maybe there's a homeless kitchen somewhere we could give it to.

Tessa   Wouldn't let us. Fucking health and safety. For the homeless! Incredible.

Michael   We could start up our own. 'You eat what he doesn't' . . .

Tessa   It would only give you incentive.

Tessa *pushes the pizza away from her with a groan.*

Tessa   My throat is sore.

She lies her torso across the table like a dead body. She sighs dramatically. She writhes around, groaning. She can't seem to get comfortable. She makes a show of all this for **Michael***.*

Michael *rises and goes to the television, switching it on. He watches it, leaning against the counter.*

Tessa *rises and switches it off. She shoots* **Michael** *a look before returning to her seat.*

Michael *rises and turns the television on. He stays beside it.*

Tessa *rises and turns it off. She stays with him.*

Michael *turns it on.* **Tessa** *turns it off.* **Michael** *turns it on.*

Tessa *hauls herself onto the counter, sitting herself directly in front of the screen, obscuring it from view. Reaching her hand behind her back, she turns it off.*

Michael *fetches his Sudoku book from the counter and holds it up to her before sitting down to work on a puzzle.*

Tessa *bores holes in his head with her eyes.*

Tessa   Is this what you did all day? No work, no wife, just Sudoku and black coffee? Fucking sad.

No response from **Michael***.*

Tessa   Fucking pathetic.

No response from **Michael***.*

Tessa   Don't bury your head in the sand, Michael, put up a fight at least.

Michael   To sate your boredom?

Tessa   To regrow a spine! Some testicles maybe!

Michael *returns to his Sudoku.*

Tessa   It's amazing I fell for you in the first place.

Michael What were you thinking.

Tessa I don't know.

Michael *doesn't respond.*

Tessa Actually it was your intelligence. You were very smart, you may remember. I could have such *con-ver-sations* with you.

Michael *focuses on his Sudoku.*

Tessa So where's that man I married?

Michael (*calmly, joking, not raising his head*)   You ate him.

A pause.

Tessa That oily taste is back. It's the worst part of this whole thing.

No response from **Michael**.

Tessa (*nodding towards his Sudoku puzzle*)   . . . Easy Medium or Hard?

Michael (*checking the corner of the page*)   Fiendish.

Tessa Almost finished?

Michael Not even close.

Tessa Hurry up.

Michael *looks at her.*

Tessa I'm waiting.

Michael *turns away from her in his seat.*

Tessa That's right, do that, you can do that, that's easy.

No response from **Michael**.

Tessa Just block me out.

Pause.

I suppose this happens to everyone. At some point. Couples always end up hating each other, my parents did. You just sped things up a bit. But it's pretty common, wouldn't you say. Ordinary, I'd imagine. Though of course, not everyone's husband has an eating disorder. That's a bit of spice. You've always had that particular talent for making it all about you.

Michael That's funny, here I was thinking it was all about you.

Tessa   Me? This isn't about me –

Michael   Oh yes it is.

Tessa   It's about you.

Michael   Sure.

Tessa   You're just too self-absorbed to see it.

Michael   That doesn't make sense, Tessa.

Tessa   Yes it does. You want to be a martyr, and no one can be a guilty martyr, so it *can't* be about *you*, because then *you* would be to blame. So of *course* it's about me!

Michael   I'm sure at least part of it is about Jack.

Tessa *doesn't respond.*

Michael   Don't you agree?

Tessa   Part of it, of course, is about Jack. How could it not be.

Pause.

Michael   Did I tell you what Ameera said? That first morning, she said . . . You should call her.

Tessa   I'm not going to call her.

Michael   She said he was so *big*. Like there was so much of him in that tiny body, that tiny almost-a-person body. She was right – Jack brought it all together. Like a little . . . like the sun shone right through him, like a little neutron star, you remember? That documentary?

Tessa   You're talking like your old self again.

Scene 9

Tessa *is at the doorway in her coat, with bags of groceries in her fists. She sees* **Michael** *sitting at the table. They are silent for a moment because on the table are two plates and two sandwiches – one for* **Tessa** *and one half eaten.*

Tessa *looks at* **Michael** *questioningly.*

Michael   I'm sorry, I only managed half.

Tessa   You ate a sandwich?

Michael   I just had an urge. Thought I should take advantage while I had it, by the time you came home it might have gone.

Beat.

So I made you one.

Tessa *sits slowly, looking at her sandwich in disbelief.*

Tessa   How much did you have?

Michael   About half.

Tessa   How many bites?

Michael   Four, say.

Tessa   Were they big?

Michael   Um, medium?

Tessa *picks up the sandwich and brings it to eye level. She slowly sinks her teeth into it and groans with pleasure. She chews and rolls her eyes, smiling, through the food she says:*

Tessa   Thank you.

Tessa *then begins to eat more rapidly, chewing and biting without pause.*

Michael   Uh, be careful, not too fast.

Tessa *ignores him.*

Michael   The body, it finds it hard to . . .

At that point **Tessa** *halts, her eyes suddenly wide and she stops eating. She spits out what she has in her mouth and rushes to the sink. She vomits into it.* **Michael** *sighs heavily.* **Tessa** *does not raise her head, but cries into the sink, leaning her body into it.*

Michael   You can have the rest later, you only had half, so there's half left. It'll still count, take a break, come back to it.

Tessa (*not raising her head*)   Why didn't you tell me?

Michael   I tried to.

Tessa   Too late!

Michael   I thought you'd at least be happy I'd eaten a sandwich!

Tessa (*looking at him*)   But I can't!

Michael   Yes you can! I've just said / . . .!

Tessa   I'm losing, always losing . . .

Michael   There's nothing to lose!

Tessa   Except this stupid game of yours.

Michael   Of mine?!

Tessa   And a bit of weight.

Michael   And a bit of pride.

Tessa   You think this is for pride!

Michael   I don't know what this is, but I know it's not for me!

Tessa   Of course it's for you, it's only for you that I'm here at all!

Michael   You know, you tell me that every day but there has been no attempt, no hint of reconciliation!

Tessa   How can you say that! This is all to – We have to sort things out, don't we! I came back to do that!

Michael   Well you haven't! Have you! You just make me feel like shit and love doing it and I look for your help, Tessa, I keep my eye out for it but all I actually see is not your help, but your spite and your cruelty and your guilt and your hate!

Tessa   You think I hate you?

Michael (*measured*)   I think / –

Tessa   You think I hate you?

Michael (*roars*)   Stop interrupting me!

(*short pause*) I don't know what I think! Anymore! Do you love me? Are you here to help me? Or is this . . . If you do not love me, cannot love me, leave me. Because I. Do not. Need this. You understand. I do not, need this.

Tessa   Yes you do.

Michael   No, you do! You're here to purge your sins, aren't you! You blame and you blame and you blame and you blame me but really this is some fucking backwards confessional.

Tessa   For what!

Michael   For leaving the way you did! Without a word! For asking your brother to beat me if he saw me! Yes he told me! For changing your number! At least you came to the funeral, but not the wake! And everyone was asking me and I didn't know because you wouldn't tell me! I am not punishing myself, I've done that, you're just getting started. And what a way to do it – get me to hold your hand through it, show you how it's done, and all the while you can accuse / me of holding the whip! –

Tessa   Stop analysing me!

Michael   – It's perfect! You can get the comeuppance you crave because you know you need / it –

Tessa   *I* need punishment?!

Michael   – Without ever admitting deserving it!

Tessa   You're the fucking murderer!

A heavy pause. **Michael** *sits down.* **Tessa** *is uneasy.*

Tessa   I'm sorry.

Michael   It's ok.

Pause.

Michael   Eat your sandwich. Slowly.

Tessa *sits down to the sandwich, and takes a very slow bite out of it.* **Michael** *watches her.*

Scene 10

Michael *stands at the counter with two glasses and a bag of sugar. He stirs the sugar into the two glasses of water, dissolving it.* **Tessa** *lies on the floor, clutching her stomach.*

Tessa   I thought I'd feel better. I don't. I feel worse.

Michael   This will help.

Tessa   But I think I'm past the point of . . . not caring, but . . . needing to care. You know?

Michael   No.

Tessa   So, I'm not tracking how many meals I'm skipping in a day anymore, it's just . . . well dinner I notice because I keep making it, but . . . you know. Am I being coherent?

MORE.

Michael   No. But that might be me not being able to concentrate, not you being incoherent.

Tessa   I mean, it's easier now but I still want to stop.

Michael (*bringing the glasses to the table*)   It's like OCD kind of, for me. You hate doing it but you have to do it. Or wanking when you're just starting out.

Tessa (*completely dumbfounded*)   What?

Michael   You know, when you – actually I guess you might not. Um, when guys start, masturbating, they – well *I* got really guilty afterwards and felt terrible, but it didn't make me not do it again later.

Tessa   Well that / aside . . .

Michael   I suppose a drug simile would have been better.

Tessa   Yes. That aside this is taking quite a bit of motivation.

Michael   I have a mantra.

Tessa   You never told me that.

Michael   No, I didn't.

Tessa   I want to hear it.

Michael *looks at her to make sure.*

Tessa (*smiling*)   Maybe it'll help.

Beat.

Michael   Quod me nutrit me destruit.

Tessa (*translating*)   What nourishes me destroys me.

Michael   Angelina Jolie has it as a tattoo, I think.

Tessa   Latin's a dead language.

Michael   But it's on such a beautiful body.

Tessa   You look nothing like her.

Michael (*ignoring her*)   If you think about it, it brings a whole new light to what we're doing. People were talking about this 3,000 years ago, putting it into poetry / . . .

Tessa   Just because it's old doesn't mean it's right. It's not natural, even the Romans gorged themselves / and –

Michael   This is good, I miss this.

Tessa   – And lions, when they kill, their bellies drag along the floor.

Michael   Tattoos aren't natural. Piercings aren't natural. But they all make you a bit special, don't they. We're special.

Tessa   You know I have been doing my research. Swotting up on a-noh-rec-see-ah.

Michael   Oh really?

Tessa   Really. And I discovered it's largely considered a middle-class disease, which is quite tedious and means we pretty much fit the bill there, but did you know that out of all anorexics, only twenty per cent are male?

Michael   Yes I did.

Tessa   So you are special. Like a Panda.

They share a laugh.

Michael   An endangered species.

Tessa   Well, just a rarity.

Michael   No, I mean, you know eighty five per cent of that twenty per cent die?

Tessa   What?

Michael   Oh that wasn't in your textbook, student Tess?

Tessa   Die from what?

Michael   Mis-diag-nosis.

Beat.

But no fear there, is there. Silver lining.

Tessa (*sighing*)   You know all the forums talk about body dysmorphia –

Michael   Ooh big word.

Tessa   – why can't you just have that? Things would be so much easier, I could just say you weren't fat and be done with it.

Michael   Didn't work for my mother, did it.

Tessa   Well she's an idiot. And she doesn't know about Sarah Queens.

Michael   Ugh thank god.

Tessa   Sarah Queeeeeeeeens!

Michael   You're just jealous.

Tessa   Most teenagers just scratch at their wrists with their dad's razor when their girlfriend fucks someone else.

Michael   Not my girlfriend.

Tessa   Oh that's right! You couldn't even get her in / the first place!

Michael   And I had my own razor thank you.

Tessa   Oh? What have you done with it?

Michael (*referring to his beard/stubble*)   Don't you like it? I thought it was rugged.

Tessa   'Sarah Queens! Will you love me if I'm rugged?'

Michael   Good idea, should have given that a shot.

Tessa   'Sarah Queens! Will you love me if I'm skin and bones?'

Michael   Hey I was always skinny.

Tessa   I've seen the pictures.

Michael   Always toyed with dieting, pushing myself, it's always / been . . . [a part of me]

Tessa   But that was the first time you stopped completely.

Michael   Sure.

Tessa   Right. To prove your love.

Michael   To prove my . . . self. To myself.

I wasn't . . . in my head it was like I was taking something back. It was like I was stronger. Because I could win at that. She could see how strong I was and feel . . . / terrible.

Tessa   Overcome with regret and come running to your arms.

Michael   Uh, no.

Tessa   Look don't deny it, Michael, it's too obvious.

Michael   That's not what I was doing.

Tessa   And now you're doing it again!

Michael   No I'm not.

Tessa   You stopped eating to win her back, just like me.

Michael   I didn't want her back. She'd been, spoiled. And I'm not trying to get you back either.

Tessa   Don't lie.

Beat.

Michael   I'm not.

Beat.

Sorry but I'm not.

Tessa   Why not.

Michael   I don't see much point. As I said, you're not exactly, encouraging.

Tessa   No.

Beat.

Michael   So.

Tessa   But. To be fair. I am here. So that's, something. Isn't it?

Michael   That is something.

They both drink.

Scene 11

More dishes sitting around the kitchen. All the smells are starting to meld together and stink. **Tessa** *is wearing an apron and watching a cooking programme and miming along with a chopping board and knife.* **Michael** *is watching her from the doorway, she never takes her eyes off the screen.*

Michael   What are you doing?

Tessa   Practicing.

Michael   Aren't you going to cook later?

Tessa   I miss doing it for lunch, so I'm pretending.

Michael *sits down at the table and starts twisting his wrist, looking at it.*[1]

Tessa   It's hard though because my fingers are numb, and I'm having trouble focusing on the screen, it's too bright, it's bleeding off into star shapes around the edges.

Michael   Means you're getting worse.

Tessa *brings herself away from the television when the adverts begin and joins him at the table, turning the screen off as she does. She smiles.*

Tessa   I feel better today though.

Michael   Good.

Michael *continues curling his wrist.* **Tessa** *watches him.*

Tessa   What *is* that?

Michael   What?

Tessa   What you're doing.

Michael   Oh. Measuring.

Tessa   Your wrist?

Michael *nods.*

Tessa   Are you buying a bracelet?

Michael   I'm tracking progress. Bones, veins, thickness generally. The aim is to get the whole arm as thin as this bit.

Michael *demonstrates, pointing to his wrist.*

Tessa   It'll get that thin?

Michael   Almost.

A pause, **Tessa** *contemplates this.*

Tessa   What else will happen?

Michael   What do you mean?

Tessa   Well I'm slimming but what else?

Michael   Look it up.

Tessa   But I've got an expert of the field in my kitchen.

---

1   Michael may have done this action earlier in the play, it is a slight physical tick of his.

Michael   *Your* kitchen?

Tessa *snarls at him.* **Michael** *considers it, then turns to face her fully, taking a deep breath.*

Michael   Well, now this is only how I had it, so I don't know if it happens every time to everybody. But . . . well first off there's the headaches and lightheadedness.

Tessa   Check.

Michael   Weight loss is a given.

Tessa   Of course.

Michael   And then . . . so there's hunger, but there'll be a point where you push past it. But just before that your stomach will rumble all the time and really loudly. And it starts to ache and you can feel every movement and, well, everything. You feel everything. Are you . . . have you got that?

Tessa   Yeah that's it exactly. But maybe I'm overreacting because I don't know what to expect.

Michael   Well anyway, then it'll break and there'll be a – relief. It's like . . . it's hard to describe, but . . . the only thing I can liken it to is being trapped in the worst nightclub ever with seven strobes all going at once and finally – walking out. Into a garden. And from then on, you just feel . . . great. Honestly, it's – amazing. And it's easier after that, and you feel like nothing hurts and nothing can hurt you.

(*takes a breath*) Then, when your BMI gets below a certain level, your muscles are the first thing to go. Everyone knows that. You eat them, basically, because the body hasn't got any fat anymore. Body hair stops growing. Mine just got downy really, but like on your chest – well not *your* chest but, pubic hair and hair that's stimulated by hormones – because they get seriously messed up – it stops growing. Falls out sometimes.

Not enough protein to keep it stuck to your scalp. Your teeth lose colour and get brittle because they're underused. There's an oil in your mouth all the time and it makes you stink. The chemical that regulates emotions gets fucked too, you can't feel anything, mentally, now. There's no real sadness, no real joy, just fluctuations from the middle. You can't concentrate. You can't communicate what you mean. Like having a stroke, unable to get at the words in your head – it's like that.

A heavy silence.

Michael   In terms of internal organs I don't know, but remember that girl on the drip? Her stomach couldn't process food anymore.

Tessa   What about periods?

Michael   Oh – yeah. Forgot about that, understandably. Um . . . you'll stop. Have you already?

Tessa   I don't know, I'm not due, though I am soon.

Michael   So we'll soon find out.

Tessa   . . . Is that permanent?

Michael   . . . I don't know.

Tessa *chews her lip and starts miming again.*

Tessa   . . . Well, that just means I'm not cutting you any slack with dinner tonight, no matter how big a half-sandwich you ate the other day.

Michael   Ok.

Beat.

I feel like you're trying to get me to eat my broccoli. Choo Choo, chugga chugga chugga chugga . . .

Tessa   Jack set a good example and always gave in.

Michael   Well, he was four. Easy to manipulate.

Tessa   Almost four.

Tessa *stops miming.*

Tessa   I miss him, so . . . I can't believe it sometimes. That I can miss him, so . . .

Michael   I hate walking by his room. Have you been in?

Tessa   I can't.

Michael   Don't feel like you have to, you don't.

Tessa   Have you?

Michael   A few times. To get rid of the dust.

Tessa   . . . Thank you for taking care of that.

Pause.

Tessa   I want to go up there.

Michael   . . . You're sure?

Tessa   Very.

Michael   . . . Ok.

Michael *stands.* **Tessa** *follows suit. They stand looking at each other.*
Tessa *is breathing heavily.* **Michael** *reaches out his hand to comfort her,*
and **Tessa** *walks to the door, stopping at the threshold. She takes big*
gulps of air, leaning on the door frame. **Michael** *watches her, unsure of*
what to do. She half-turns to him, not looking at him, but presenting her
hand for him to hold. He takes it. They walk out.

Scene 12

Michael *and* **Tessa** *are sitting in their places at the table, with a plate of*
hot stew in front of them. It is evening.

Michael *lifts a fork-full and puts it in his mouth.* **Tessa** *is surprised and*
elated and eagerly puts a fork-full in her own mouth. They sit, looking at
each other, not moving, **Tessa** *hopeful and smiling.*

Michael *is the first to chew, which he does slowly like a cow. He*
swallows, then opens his mouth to show **Tessa**. *She copies him,*
gleeful.

Tessa *and* **Michael** *continue to raise their forks to their mouths in*
unison, placing their food on their tongues, chewing, then **Tessa** *waits*
for **Michael** *to swallow and open his mouth to show her it's gone before*
doing so herself.

This happens again, but **Michael** *grimaces apologetically at* **Tessa**.
Tessa *is disappointed, but sighs compliance and* **Michael** *lets his food*
fall off of his tongue and onto the plate.

The hanging light above them blows out. They stare at it.

Michael   Huh.

Tessa   Do we have more?

Michael   Yeah.

Michael *walks over to the kitchen sink, opening the cupboard*
underneath it and producing a lightbulb box. **Tessa** *nods and* **Michael**
goes to turn off the light at the switch.

Tessa *climbs straight from her chair onto the table to reach the lightbulb, but from the sudden change in height and lack of food she is dizzy and stumbles.* **Michael** *runs to support her round the waist until she has her bearings again.*

Tessa *exhales dramatically and smiles down at him, mumbling thanks. He is equally non-specific in his reply. They seem happy.*

Michael *hands her the lightbulb and she screws it in, passing the used one to him.* **Michael** *turns on the light and it blinks on. They celebrate mildly.*

Michael *puts the plates by the sink and* **Tessa** *lowers herself down to sit on the table, back to the audience.*

Michael *returns from the counter and hops up beside her, also facing away from the audience.*

Tessa   Is it one of those energy saving ones?

Michael   Yeah.

Tessa (*approving*)   Huh.

They swing their legs together.

Scene 13

Tessa *and* **Michael** *are lying on the table, lights still on, a little askew but fully clothed, having obviously fallen asleep there. Their bodies spoon each other,* **Michael**'s *arm around her waist.*

Tessa *shifts in her sleep and wakes slowly. She sees* **Michael** *beside her and smiles to herself. She reaches to his hand and takes it in hers, drawing it closer to her.*

Scene 14

Michael *is sitting at the table, facing towards the door. His head is bent down over a Sudoku puzzle.* **Tessa** *storms in with two full plastic bags of shopping, fuming, though* **Michael** *doesn't notice as he doesn't raise his head from his Sudoku book.*

Michael (*not looking up*)   Hello.

Tessa *throws the shopping bags at him.*

Michael   What?!

Tessa   The sandwich!

Michael   What?

Tessa   The sandwich!

Michael *tries to collect up the groceries from the table and the floor, avoiding eye contact with* **Tessa***.*

Michael   What do you mean, I don't understand / you . . .

Tessa   That fucking sandwich that fucking fake fucking sandwich! Well I fucking found it didn't I!

Michael   What?

Tessa (*mocking*)   What what what what what what what!

Tessa *takes the items* **Michael** *has collected and throws them back at him, around him, everywhere.*

Michael   Stop, stop it! Stop it!

Tessa   You thought I wouldn't find it! You're so fucking stupid, you stupid – I don't sit in the house all day with fucking Sudoku like you fucking do, I go out and have to be recognized and fucking chatted to and have all those fucking condolences heaped on me and come back to you, my fucking dying morose fucking husband, who can't even *pretend* to eat a fucking sandwich! –

Michael   Tess . . .

Tessa   – But then I thought, I was thinking, surely, *surely* he can't be *that* fucking dumb, I did like him enough, think highly enough of him to marry him in the first fucking place. –

Michael   I'm so / – [sorry]

Tessa   – So why, *why* would he leave half a fucking sandwich in the fucking bushes, why didn't he just make half a sandwich? Why didn't he / . . .

Michael   You would have known.

Tessa (*thrown*)   What?

Michael   If I used one slice of bread you would have seen the two ends. I had to take the bites out of the whole sandwich. And you'd probably notice that I hadn't used enough ingredients too.

Tessa   . . . So you took the bites and spat them out in the bushes?

Michael   Yes.

Pause.

Tessa *throws another item and* **Michael** *reacts very little, only flinching on its impact, keeping his eyes to the ground.*

Tessa   You knew I'd see it, I'd notice. Birds were eating it, the ants led me to it. It's horrible, all disintegrated . . . Quod me nutrit me destruit! Is this what you meant!

(*exaggerating now, hyperbolic*) You've *destroyed* me! I'm *vanquished*! Like fucking *Eve*, you fucking snake!

Michael   I was trying to help/.

Tessa   Bullshit! You were trying to make a fool out of me! I am not a fucking fool!

Michael   I was just – trying – to make you eat.

Tessa   And I'm just trying to make you eat and I'm not being underhanded about it!

Michael   This isn't a sport, Tessa!

Tessa   But you owe it to me to play by the rules.

Michael   And you owe me some compassion. But you've been completely callous since Jack went!

Tessa   Nobody went. He didn't get taken to a farm where he can have open fields and chase rats all day, he's not a puppy, he died, Michael. And yes, death has an affect on people sometimes, and I guess I didn't go out and buy one of those tiny fucking 'poems for sadness' books like everyone else.

Michael   Neither did I but I also didn't turn into a harpy!

Tessa   Oh and you're so noble for it!

Michael   Oh but I'm not. People lose people every day . . .

Tessa   Don't you dare! Don't you dare treat it like everyone else because he was not everyone else, he was mine! He was my Jack! He was my Jack! He was my! Jack!

Michael   And mine!

Pause.

Tessa   I wanted to vomit. When I found out. About the sandwich, I mean, I wanted to bring it all up, to make us even again. But then I realized, I couldn't. There would just be bile, just liquid, because that sandwich was days ago. So you've won, Michael, well done / tu gagnes –

Michael   Don't be stupid, Tess . . .

Tessa   – Michael: Un Point.

Michael   Tessa . . .

Tessa   Tessa: Nil Points!

Michael   Look I was doing it for you and you know it. But you can't handle the kindness so you chalk it up to competition, something you're much more comfortable with.

Tessa   Eat a sandwich or I'm taking a laxative.

Michael   What?

Tessa   Eat a sandwich or I'm taking a laxative.

Michael   That'll fuck up your stomach, it'll be terrible.

Tessa   Not worse than starving myself, surely.

Michael   Yes worse!

Tessa *shrugs.*

Michael *tries to stare her down but fails.*

Michael   What am I supposed to do?

Tessa *is silent.*

Michael   Ok.

Pause.

Michael   Take the laxative.

Tessa *defiantly rifles in her shopping bag and takes out a sheet of pills. She pops two out and tries to swallow them without water. She can't.*

She pushes past him to run herself a glass of water. She gulps the pills down, slams the glass on the counter and storms out of the room, her footsteps heavy up the stairs.

Michael *rubs his forehead. He is stressed.*

He taps the counter. He jostles his haunches.

He replaces the chair at its place at the table. He takes time over getting its position exactly right in relation to the table. He does the same for the other chair.

He looks around the room.

He opens his Soduko book and tries to work on a puzzle but can't.

He gets a glass from a cupboard and pours sugar into it. He goes to the sink for water but stops, changing his mind and dumping the sugar into the sink.

Scene 15

Michael *and* **Tessa** *are sitting opposite each other, plates of shepherd's pie in front of them.* **Tessa** *is wearing a nightgown and looks obviously weak.*

Michael   You look awful.

Tessa *is silent.*

Michael   Drink something at least.

Tessa *does not respond.*

Michael *throws his fork across the table at* **Tessa** *'s plate.* **Tessa** *is surprised, but does nothing.*

Michael   I realized something. It's very important, do you want to hear it? I realized I have a clean criminal record. Do you realize that?

Beat.

I have never been in jail, or prosecuted for theft, rape, anything. Even murder. Or wrongful neglect.

Beat.

You never took me to court. Because you knew it wasn't my fault.

Tessa   You *were* his father.

Michael   But you couldn't do it. You never could actually accuse me. You know really I'm not, accountable . . .

Tessa   Do I? Do I really? You know what, I don't, because I don't know, I don't understand how anyone can give their seriously / . . .

Michael   I know.

Tessa   *Seriously* intolerant son / a . . .

Michael   I know! I / –!

Tessa   Without checking / first!

Michael   But I / –!

Tessa   Without even / checking first!

Michael   Well *I* did, didn't I!

Tessa   Without / –!

Michael (*roaring*)   But I did! I did I did! I did, didn't I! I did, I did that, I did it, I did. I did and I'm sorry. I am sorry. And I've said it before and over and over and I *am* sorry! I am! I'm sorry!

Tessa   I don't believe you. Look at you. You're watching TV. You're playing Sudoku.

Michael   I'm starving myself!

Tessa   It's too easy! You're too good at it! Just, sitting back and wasting away, it's not fair!

Michael   Fair? Don't! I lost the two people I love, more than anything, at once! In the space of three days he was gone and so were you! Is that fair? I had to deal with it all on my own, is that fair? Had to wake up in the middle of the night, his face in my dreams –

Tessa   Don't tell me.

Michael   – His neck as thick as his shoulders –

Tessa   Stop it.

Michael   – Still hearing him gargling nonsense like in those churches, like in rapture –

Tessa   I don't want to know!

Michael   – Telling him every night it's going to be ok. Thrashing the pillow in my sleep, trying to squeeze it out of him, leaving finger marks – and yes! Alright! The guilt! My! Guilt! All on my own! Is it fair, that the person you love, who's always been the one to drag you up and stop you drowning, leaves you. Can't understand, can't see it was an accident! Can't forgive you!

Tessa   How do I forgive you! Tell me how! Please! Just looking at you, it makes me . . . You're this monster! And you're lucky! I could have done so much more. You have no idea, do you. What I wanted to do! To you! To myself! What I could have done! Pulled out my hair and my eyelashes! My toenails! Set fire to myself! Run naked into traffic! Screamed until my lungs came up! Jumped off the tallest building and no one would have been surprised! I could have done anything!

(*choking back tears*) And I'm doing something, here, now, I'm doing something. And you're doing something too, you're ignoring it.

Michael   I'm not.

Beat.

I can't get better. You must know that. I don't deserve to. Please, stop asking me to.

Silence.

Tessa (*whispering, to herself*)   Choo choo, choo choo . . .

Tessa *suddenly thrusts her hand forward and pushes the food into his mouth.* **Michael** *tries to retreat but is trapped –* **Tessa** *holds her palm over his lips and the other on the back of his head.* **Michael** *gags and jerks.*

He gulps, finally swallowing. After making certain he won't regurgitate it, she releases her back hand to stroke his face and he shoves her away from him. She slams against the table.

Michael *snatches the plate. He scoops some into his hand. He repeats her actions, she struggles but submits, and he makes sure she keeps the food down.*

Tessa *takes another handful.* **Michael** *jolts back. They silently negotiate, both afraid. She feeds* **Michael** *again. He lets her.*

Michael *sits down on the table, then lies down.* **Tessa** *feeds him as he lies. He swallows, looking up at her.*

Tessa *covers his mouth and nose, and he sputters for air. He lashes out and tries to free himself but cannot. Eventually* **Michael**'s *struggle stops and he slowly lowers his arms, submitting.* **Tessa** *sees this and is touched, but defiantly continues.*

Eventually **Tessa** *breaks down and releases him.* **Michael** *gulps for air as she falls down onto him, their faces touching. They run their hands over each other's faces, through each other's hair, around each other's necks. They stumble into a kiss, broken by moaning, then wailing, then with little screams as they lie together, convulsing with grief.*

Scene 16

It is late night and dark.

Michael *enters in the darkness, looking around a little before sitting down at the table.*

After a few moments, the light from the hallway clicks on and **Tessa** *trudges through the kitchen door. She sees* **Michael***, illuminated by the hall light.*

A shameful pause.

Tessa   You couldn't sleep either.

Michael   I could, hear you . . .

Tessa *exhales bashfully.*

Tessa   Do you, uh . . . I was thinking, do you want to – move back into your room?

Michael   . . . Maybe not tonight.

Tessa   Ok, yeah, yeah that's smart.

Michael   But, thank you.

Tessa *looks around her. She walks to the piles of dishes and picks a few up.* **Michael** *joins her. As she scrapes food from them into the bin, he rinses them in the sink, piling them up in a tower on the side. This takes some time.*

Tessa *watches* **Michael***. She puts her arms around his waist from behind and embraces him.*

Once this is done, **Michael** *opens the door to the fridge. The light from inside illuminates him. He holds the door open.* **Tessa** *joins him in the light.*

As he reaches inside all lights go out.

Skin A Cat

For myself

Note on the Text

My experience of sex never matched up with what I saw in film, television, books, or the stage. Particularly where virginity was concerned, I was baffled as to how all the drama was in the lead up to the act, but not during. For me it had been the opposite. Not sexy. Not fun. Not what I expected or was taught would happen if I'd chosen the right dude to Do It with. I remember watching the movie *Kinsey* with my first proper boyfriend and both of us leaning forward in our seats when the primary couple is told by their doctor that there's a solution for their painful intercourse, but of course the camera cut straight to a blissful and giggling post-coitus, with no detail about what they'd done to achieve it (and of course frantic Googling afterwards wasn't fruitful either). So in a way this play is the missing part of the film I wished I'd seen at sixteen. Almost a decade later I figured that if we still weren't talking about how uneasy sex could be for some people (a surprising number in fact) then I probably should.

So I did. The whole play was very easy to write, but the script still suffered from what I now think was symptomatic of the story it told – I sent it to every venue and company I could, and most feedback was geared towards making the play something different to what it was, making it more like other plays. But I was by this point very clear that the whole point was that this play was not and should not be like other plays, because this story was not like other stories, and that's why it was important to me to tell it. When Blythe Stewart read it and immediately understood this I practically fell over myself in begging her to direct it. This turned out to be a smart move, because with grit, favours, our own bank accounts, our own bedding as set and the costume designer's own bra in the costume, we brought *Skin A Cat** to the VAULT Festival, sold out every night, and were given the Pick Of The Year Award before being offered the opening slot of the brand new Bunker Theatre.

I wish I could tell my fifteen- to twenty-five-year-old self that one day all this horrible vagina stuff was going to make a great play that people would praise and thank me for (praise is really the only reason I do anything). But more than that I wish I could have known then what I know now – that I was not alone, and that it would be ok. I'm very honoured to be able to, through jokes about willies and bums and flaps, tell other Alanas out there that it's going to be ok.

---

* One of the weirdest reactions I've ever received to telling someone about the particulars of my sex life was from one of my ex-boyfriend's mother, who responded with caring nonchalance: 'Well there's more than one way to skin a cat'. I'd never heard that phrase before and it took some explaining, but it was (in so many ways) perfect.

Thanks

To Playdate (CA, PC, SK, SL, VP, DR) and Crowther Club (JB, SH, AW) for letting me sob on their shoulders and always being first in the ticket line. To Inua Ellams and Leo Butler for knowing the value of a good quote from a good name. To Tell Tales (EK, FK, GM) and IdeasTap Takeover: Love (GB, FF, SK, GM, KPW) for helping me test sex on stage. To Blythe Stewart for immediately and completely getting the play, and being the first to put her money where her mouth was. To the SAC Creatives (JA, JC, ID, LL, RL, HP, ZAR, HR, BS) who put literal blood sweat and tears into the production. To Peggy Ramsay for providing writers with serious support without bullshit. To Vinay Patel for the big bucks. To the private donors that got us up and running. To the VAULT Festival for being a genuine hub of genuine risk taking (and for the cool award). To all the play's early champions (SG, LK, NT, CW) for buzz and boost. To Jonathan Kinnersley for being an incredible ally. To the NHS for making everything within reach. To Marie Stopes for the play's ending. To my parents and brother who understand the need to make space for difference. To my family for inexhaustible love and pride and support. To all the friends and all the lovers who made it into this play (and those that didn't) for their overwhelming acceptance. And to Geoffrey for everything, all of it, every single bit.

We are the only authority on what is good for us. Once we see this, we feel an enormous peace and freedom.

Hugh Prather

You alone are enough.

Maya Angelou

Skin A Cat was first performed at the VAULT Festival on 27 January 2016. The cast was as follows:

Alana Lydia Larson
Women Jessica Clark
Men Jeassa Ahluwalia

Creative Team
Director Blythe Stewart
Producer Sophie Cornell for Essee Productions,
Cara McAleese, Isabelle Dixon
Scene & Costume Designer Holly Pigott
Lighting Designer Harrison Routledge
Stage Manager Holly Marsh

Skin A Cat then transferred to The Bunker in London, opening on 12 October 2016. The cast was as follows:

Alana Lydia Larson
Women Jessica Clark
Men Jeassa Ahluwalia

Creative Team
Director Blythe Stewart
Producer Zoë Robinson for RIVE Productions
Scene & Costume Designer Holly Pigott
Lighting Designer Harrison Routledge
Stage Manager Kristy Bowers

Skin A Cat toured the UK in 2018. Cast as follows:

Alana Lydia Larson
Women Libby Rodliffe
Men Joe Eyre

Creative Team
Director Blythe Stewart
Producer Zoë Robinson for RIVE Productions
Scene & Costume Designer Holly Pigott
Lighting Designer Lucy Adams

Characters

Alana, *ages 9–25, played by someone 25 or older, very plain*
Mother, *Alana's mother*
Jess, *15*
Simon, *17*
Kevin, *19*
Nathaniel, *16*
Peter, *16–19*
Sally, *18–23*
Johnny, *18–23*
Mark, *20s*
Doctor, *female, 30s*
Gerry, *50s*
Waitress, *20s*
Psychiatrist, *female, 40*

Suggested Doubling, *Alana plays herself, one actor plays all male characters, one actor plays all female characters*

A Note

This play is unashamedly autobiographical. That said, not all of it is true. I'll happily answer any questions that come up with regards to its staging, production, etc. Please don't hesitate to ask them.

Key

If a character's line ends with— and their next lines begins with — then the lines run on as one without pause
/ marks a point of interruption
Interrupted lines are still spoken in their entirety
[ ] indicates speech which is not said out loud but is included to clarify the intention of the line

A bed.

Alana *enters, sees the bed.*

Alana (*to the audience*)   Oh, this is – I thought – no I guess that's a cliché.

Sits.

Comfy. We won't have to . . . will we? No, good, ok then. Lovely. Sorry, I'm . . . nervous. But I'm, fully up for it.

Definitely. And look just before I get started I just wanted to say something. I want to . . . This is really hard for me. This is what I've spent the last – a long time – . . . this is basically my worst nightmare. Um. But I'm going to try. Because I think it's a good idea. So I'll just – [start]? Shall I?
I'm going to try and tell you everything. I'm going to try.
Ok. Um. Right.
I don't actually know where to start . . .
Yes I do.

Mother   Excuse me, do you have a pad on you? A sanitary pad? No? Thank you. Excuse me, you don't happen to have a pad on you? For women? I'm sorry, excuse me, I'm trying to get hold of a pad – feminine emergency. No, a tampon won't do I'm afraid. Thanks anyway. Excuse me, I'm sorry to interrupt, I was just wondering if anyone in your party had a pad, like a sanitary pad? No? Would you mind asking around? No no, I really need a pad.

Alana   My mum's on holiday, on an island resort, and she's trying to find someone, anyone with a pad she can use. It's not for her. It's for me, back at the cabin with a folded wad of toilet paper wedged into my pants. I'm nine years old, and I'm having my first period.

I don't remember how I discovered it exactly . . . I remember the chaos that followed. Dad wasn't there. I mean, ever, he wasn't around. Never met him, and never wanted to, really. Easier. I figured if he hadn't been in touch he obviously didn't want to be. Or maybe he was dead. Anyway eventually one of the dive masters gave her some and by the next day they had all pooled their resources and come up with a rainbow of different brands for me to use. I thought that was fun, at first. But then I realized that my becoming a woman was ruining my mum's holiday a bit.

We did not talk about it. I had no idea what was going on. I felt very – wrong. Very bad. Why was this happening? Was I sick? Was I broken?

Why wouldn't Mum talk to me? Why didn't she want anyone else talking to me either? Why did she look at her menu so much, out at the sea so much, at me so little? Why did she finish the books she brought so quickly? I was left to figure it all out by myself.

Mother   No more swimming.

Alana   That's all she told me. So I studied what was left on the scratchy pads every few hours – red blood, yes, but brown too, and sometimes like clumps of jam. Sometimes little stringy aliens, stranded on the padding. They looked like biro marks, when you're not really writing you're just thinking, or on the telephone – my mum does that a lot, doodling her conversation. But now, she was silent and her hands were very still.

I thought this was going to be the way things were, forever, from here on out. I'll be bleeding for the rest of my life. I thought I'd never see my friends again. I thought maybe

I was a witch – and that was a little exciting at first, I'll admit, but not after the first few days.

Thankfully, it stopped. Then started. Then stopped again and started again and I ruined a few good dresses before my mum sat on my bed with me and said:

Mother   It's called getting your period.

Alana (*to* **Mother**)   What is it?

Mother   It's menstruation.

Alana   What's that?

Mother   It's natural.

Alana   Oh.

Mother   Everybody does it.

Alana   Everybody?

Mother   Every girl.

Alana   Boys?

Mother   Not boys.

Alana   Not boys?

Mother   No.

Alana   Weird.

Mother   So there's nothing to worry about. –

Alana   But / . . .

Mother   – It's perfectly fine, bound to happen one day. –

Alana   But / . . .

Mother   – You were just early, of course.

Alana   But what's happening?

Mother (*sighs*)   Inside you – there are – you know where eggs come from?

Alana   Chickens?

Mother   Yes, well, you're / . . .

Alana   I've got chickens?

Mother   No, you're like a chicken.

Alana   No I'm not.

Mother   Because you've got eggs too.

Alana   . . . What?

Mother   Inside you.

Alana (*beat*)   How do we get them out?

Mother   They're coming out now.

Alana   In the –?

Mother   Yes.

Alana   Doesn't look like eggs.

Mother   That's because they're so tiny you can't see them.

Alana   But why am I bleeding?

Mother   Because – because every egg has a little cushion, and when it comes out it takes the cushion with it and that's where all the blood comes from.

Alana   Like a water bed.

Mother   Exactly.

Alana (*to the audience*)   I had been begging for a water bed. (*To* **Mother**.) Can't I just – keep them inside?

Mother   No.

Alana   Why not.

Mother   You just can't.

Alana   But why can't I?

Mother   Because then you'd be full of eggs!

Alana   I don't mind.

Mother   Look – those eggs, if they stay in there, they go bad.

Alana   Why?

Mother   Because they don't turn into babies.

Alana   Babies?!

Mother   That's where babies come from, there, you might as well know.

Alana   Why don't they turn into babies?

Mother   You don't want babies do you.

Alana   Why not!

Mother   Because then you'd have to give birth!

Alana   Birth?

Mother   Oh my god, look, I'll buy you a book.

Alana (*to the audience*)   And that was that. And that was all. But now, at least, I knew: I was normal, I was full of eggs, and they wouldn't turn into babies. That was some reassurance.

I started to notice . . . lots of things. All at once it was like my legs, boobs, hips, shoulders, everything was ballooning out. More new dresses. I spent a lot of time looking in the mirror. I don't know how much is normal, but I'm pretty sure, mine was too much. But I tried to avoid . . .

She indicates her vagina.

It was the ugliest thing I'd ever seen! In my life! No wonder it's so hard to get a look at, who would want to see that every day! I don't know how it had escaped my attention until this point, but now I really took it all in and I was suddenly deeply embarrassed that my mother had seen such an awful, gross, flappy part of me. Had interacted with it, had washed it and wiped it and streaked it with ointment, had intimate knowledge of its wrinkles and folds . . . And I was ashamed that I had let her do it.

I started locking the toilet door. Mum removed the lock. I hated her for that. I hated her for a lot of things. I think most girls do, isn't that right? Their mothers, not my mother, not everyone hates my mother, just me.

Look I'm going to jump ahead a bit here because I didn't have my first boyfriend until I was 15 because my best friend was gorgeous, big boobs on top of skinny ribs so when we were out together no one paid attention to me.

Jess   Guess what.

Alana (*to* **Jess**)   What?

Jess   Guess.

Alana   No.

Jess   Go on.

Alana   I don't know, you've given up smoking.

Jess   I had sex with Si.

Alana   What!

Jess   Yeah.

Alana   What like full sex?

Jess   Full sex.

Alana   What was it like?

Jess   Incredible. I came four times. I think I'm a nymphomaniac.

Alana (*to the audience*)   She was lying. About the orgasms. It was so obvious she was lying. I knew it, at the time, I knew she was lying but I believed her anyway.
(*To* **Jess**.) Did it hurt?

Jess   Hurt? No! Of course not it was the best thing ever.

Alana   But it hurts apparently, the first time.

Jess   Well it didn't.

Alana   Not even a little bit?

Jess   I used to do horse riding, so.

Alana   Alright but, I don't know I just thought it would, hurt. You know, stretching enough so much you fit someone else inside of you. When you've never done it before.

Jess   . . . Yeah ok. Yeah a bit.

Beat.

Keep a secret?

Alana   Yeah.

Jess   . . . A lot. Actually. Blood. Don't tell anyone.

Alana (*to the audience*)   My first boyfriend, if I can call him that, he was actually her boyfriend. That, boyfriend. Si. Short for Simon. I never told her but maybe I think she knows now, I'm not sure, but at the time she didn't and I felt awful, just awful. But when your best friend's boyfriend comes up to you and says –

Simon   You're pretty.

Alana (*to the audience*)   What do you do?

Simon   Prettier than Jessie.

Alana (*to the audience*)   What do you even do?

Simon   Can I have your number?

Alana (*to the audience*)   I was fifteen. No one had ever asked me for my number before. Or said I was pretty. And friends don't count, because they're just making you feel better for being the last one in the year to get a proper kiss, everyone knows that. But. This was the guy who had just made my best friend bleed – by default, really, my only friend really – my Only Friend.

(*To* **Simon**.) Sure.

Simon   Cool. I'll prank you.

Alana (*to the audience*)   I thought maybe he was just gathering info, you know, research for when they break up, who's available, who's up for it. Laying foundations, I don't know. But two days later he texts me, asking me if I wanted to see *Bruce Almighty* with him that weekend.

I knew for a fact he and Jess had not broken up.

I said yes.

He bought himself a popcorn. He did ask if I wanted a bit. I said alright. It was sweet and I like salty but I didn't mind. And we watched the film. And I was just bringing a huge handful to my mouth when –

Simon *kisses her suddenly.*

Alana   I will not call it kissing. I mean, come on. I dropped all the popcorn on the floor. And I didn't give a fuck. Then at Jessie's sixteenth birthday – she had a house party, we all did – in her parent's bedroom, while she was downstairs . . .

Sounds of pornography. **Simon** *kisses and gropes her but* **Alana** *doesn't reciprocate.*

Simon   You're such a hot bitch. You're a hot bitch aren't you. Hot bitch. I wana put my fangars in your pussay!

Alana (*grimacing*)   It wasn't what I would have picked. I only ever watched the soft stuff, where you don't have to actually see it going in and out, you know? But that doesn't count does it. Not like the stuff Si and his mates spammed each other with. Not like what he was showing me now. This was Proper Porn.

(*To* **Simon**.) It's a bit, fast, don't you think?

(*To the audience.*) Not 'but you're going out with my best friend', not 'get the fuck off me you sweaty fucking porn weasel I wouldn't let your fingers inside me if you had cancer!' Just:

(*To* **Simon**.) Bit fast. Yeah?

Simon *sighs, rolling his eyes, and goes to* **Jess**, *spinning her around and kissing and groping her.*

Alana (*to the audience*)   But sometimes, when I'm feeling really shitty about things, I think 'What if I'd just let him . . .?'

I started drinking. I knew I was embarrassing myself but I didn't care and Jess was just as drunk as me and somehow we – she – thought it would be a good idea to / . . .

(*To* **Jess**.) I can't.

Jess   You have to.

Alana   I don't even want to . . .

Jess   Baby!

Alana   Shut up!

Jess   I have some lube here somewhere, do you want that?

Alana   What!

Jess   Might help. Make it smoother. As there's no flooow . . .

Alana (*to the audience*)   I wasn't even on my period. She just decided it was time for me to learn.

Jess   Consider it prep for your first big dick.

Alana   Is this a good idea? I'm not feeling very dexterarous – dexrous, dexterious . . .?

Jess   It's a great idea. It's easy.

Jess *produces a tampon, presenting it to* **Alana**.

It's tiny. See.

Alana   Oh my god.

Jess   Relax . . .

Alana   I can't do it. I just can't!

Jess   You haven't even tried. I've been doing it for ages and if I can do it you can do it. We'll do it together, yeah?

Jess *produces another tampon.* **Alana** *hesitates.*

It'll be fine.

Alana *groans and concedes. They both cock one leg up on the bed.*

Alana   Isn't there a diagram? Where's the diagram?

Jess   Threw it out didn't I.

Alana   I don't know what I'm doing! I need a visual aid!

Jess   No you don't you big tit, just think of, like, like a banana shape, with a weird balloon on the end. Like a tumour.

Alana   Not helping.

Jess   Count of three. One. Two . . .

Alana   I can't do this, this is all too weird and I'm too drunk I'm going to break something.

Jess   Don't be ridiculous, it's not a big deal!

Alana   It is a big deal!

Jess   All this, it's all in your head. You're freaking out. Have you had something?

Alana   I've heard they get stuck is that true? The string gets sucked up and they can't come out again . . .

Jess   Get it together!

Alana   And what about Toxic Shock Syndrome!

Jess (*hauling* **Alana** *back into position*)   One! Alright! You can do this! Two! Three!

Alana *shrieks.*

Jess   Yaaay! That wasn't so bad was it!

Alana   It's not . . . quite . . .

Jess   What?

Alana   It just . . . touched me.

Jess   Maybe I should shove it up there myself . . .

Alana   Fuck off!

Jess   Look! It's a little cotton mouse. And it's not going to hurt you. And if you don't get over this I'm going to tell everyone you're a frigid little baby who won't stick anything up her fanny.

They stare at each other.

Alana (*to the audience*)   Maybe she did know.

Jess   Take deep breaths.

Alana *reluctantly gets back into position. She inhales.*

Make sure it's angled towards your back, yeah? Don't try and force it, it'll find it's way, just gently . . . gently guide it in. Just try and un-tense all those muscles. Calm them down, just relax.

Jess *breathes slowly.*

Jess   Well?

Alana *turns to face her, releases a smile.*

Alana (*to* **Jess**)   Brilliant.

Jess   I'm so proud of you! How does it feel?

Alana   Not so bad. A bit – tight.

Jess   Soon you'll forget it's even there. Now let's go see if Darren's got weed or if Josie's a lying cow.

Alana *faces the audience. She shamefully pulls the tampon out from her waistband where she has secretly tucked it in.*

Alana (*to the audience*)   How could I have? She was right there.

That was the night I met Kevin. He was . . . good looking? I don't really know. And I don't really know how we met, or why he was there. He wasn't at our school. I think maybe he was older.

(*To herself.*) Was he . . .?

(*To the audience.*) Nope. Nothing. I just can't remember. I was – by that point, I was . . . I don't remember a fucking thing. But, I was determined. Don't remember what about, but I remember the feeling. Feeling – determined. I think that's why I drank so much, for some reason, but I'm not sure. Anyway we – somehow – ended up at his brother's house, in the spare room.

(*To* **Kevin**.) Nice.

Kevin   So like I don't know what you're up for tonight or anything but my balls are pretty fucking blue so I ain't got time for a tease, you know, I just don't got time for that / shit.

Alana   I'm not a tease.

Kevin   I wasn't sayin you was I was / just sayin . . .

Alana   And I'm not frigid.

Kevin   Cool, cool, yeah. Alright / then, well . . .

Alana   Can we just get on with it? Just straight to it?

Kevin (*beat*)   Yeah!

They get into bed.

Alana (*to the audience*)   He had a Sometimes Double. The bed, I mean. I always liked those, when I got my own bed in my first flat I made sure I got a Sometimes Double – more than enough room on your own and with someone else it forces a cuddle, or at least a spoon. But that's not what we were doing.

Kevin *reveals his erection to* **Alana**.

Alana   I was wrong. This was the ugliest thing I'd ever seen.

Kevin (*pleased*)   Yeah. You like that?

Alana   I tried to give him a hand job. But it was like a sea snake, you know those toys? The water balloon that turns in on itself? Couldn't get, a grip, or . . . kept slipping out. So I just – because it seemed easier, that's all. And so I didn't have to look at it, I just put it – [in my mouth]

Kevin   Yeah. Yeah! Yeah yeah yeah! Oh my fucking! Oh my yeah! Oh god! Oh yeah! Oh yeah! Yeeeeeaaaaah!

Alana   We held each other afterwards.

Kevin   That was fucking great.

Alana (*to* **Kevin**)   Yeah?

Kevin   Fucking beautiful.

Alana   Aw . . .

Kevin   I've like, never been this close to anyone.

Alana   Me neither.

Kevin sobs. **Alana** *comforts him, bemused but very very pleased.*

Alana (*to the audience*)   I went home the next day buzzing. Jess was going to be floored! On the bus I got a text. It was from him.

Kevin   Babe look I had fun yeah but if I'm honest I like you but I can't deal with this right now. See ya. Kev.

Alana (*beat*)   I got over it.

Beat.

Didn't see him again.

Beat.

Didn't tell Jess.

Beat.

Let's see, what's next, um . . . Pete! I didn't know Pete. Very well. He went to my school. But we met – I say met, but there was never a 'meet', just a sort of, final official acknowledgement. At school.

We went to a nice school. But there were these boys who thought they were hard. Never actually saw a fight. And their ringleader was a boy called Nathaniel. Yeah. And I remember standing in the cloisters one day and down the other end there was this younger kid, I think he wanted to take over Nathaniel's slot when we left, so he was practicing I guess and he was shouting down the other end at this guy who turned out to be Pete. I think he was calling him fat. Pete wasn't fat, but he was – soft. Rounded, not sporty, not skinny, you know? And Nathaniel hears this

and strides down the cloisters like a soldier and looms over this kid
and says:

Nathaniel   Not too smart, what you just did. Pete's the best goddamn
guy in this whole school, this whole town, and if you got a problem with
him you've got a problem with us.

Alana   Pete caught me there watching. I could tell he was embarrassed.
I smiled at him. He smiled back, kind of because that's just what you do
I think. He had nice teeth.

For some reason – maybe I just started noticing him more – we kept
bumping into each other coming in or out of the toilets, or in the canteen, or
in exams we'd clock each other. We still didn't talk. But he was in the
audience at the school drama competition at the end of term. I didn't think he
liked that sort of thing. Turns out he didn't, he was just – there to watch me.

Beat, can't stop a smile.

I won second. Points for my house, no real prizes. And honestly I think I
would have won first if I hadn't been distracted because – what was he
doing there?

Then the Easter holidays came and I got this really really long text. Do
you remember when you could only use so many characters at a time and
long messages would come through in chunks?

In the following '. . .' indicates a new text loading.

Peter   Alana, I've written this text because I need to say a few things to
you. First and foremost I'm sorry about Thursday, I didn't mean to
. . .

ignore you but I did and I'm sorry, the reason I did is because people
have been talking to me and apparently talking to you. I couldn't look at
you simply because I was so
. . .

embarrassed, I didn't know what to do or say. I think you're very
attractive and have an awesome personality and if you want to go out
with me that's great and I would be over the moon but
. . .

I don't know if I could ask you out because you're so attractive and I
know I'm no prize catch. Also you would be my first ever girlfriend and
I would screw
. . .

it up in so many ways. I've never properly kissed someone and I've never dated someone I wouldn't know what to do and I know you've already had at least one boyfriend and I

. . .

wouldn't be good enough. I love you as I love all my friends and I think you're attractive but I would not want my feelings to get in the way of our friendship, if you don't want to go out with me

. . .

that's fine, I was not expecting you to, but I want us to be friends because I think you're great and I would never want to lose such a great friend. I'm eternally sorry for avoiding you on Thursday.

Alana   I / . . .

Peter   PS I'm also sorry I couldn't say all this to your face I wanted to at least say it over MSN but you're at school doing the play and I don't know when that finishes and I don't want to interrupt.

Alana   I / . . .

Peter   PS again my birthday is on Saturday. Do you want to come to my house party? Sincerely yours, Peter.

Alana   . . . I don't remember him ignoring me. And no one had said anything to me, I have no idea what that was about. I should have texted back: 'Pete I really like you too and this is the sweetest text I've ever had, seriously, how could I say no? Don't ever think you're no prize catch, you are, you're kind and nice and sweet and lovely and I'd love to go to your party on Saturday.' But I just said: 'I'd love to come to your party on Saturday.'

(*To* **Peter**.) Hi Pete.

Peter   Hi Alana.

Alana   Happy Birthday.

Peter   Thanks.

Alana   How's it going?

Peter *shrugs, nodding.*

Alana   . . . Cool.

Awkward pause.

Peter   Do you want a drink/?

Alana   Yes.

(*To the audience.*) We drank, talked to other people, drank, watched each other from across the room while pretending not to but both knowing the other was doing the same thing, drank, drank, danced a bit, drank, until:

Peter   I'm drunk.

Alana (*to* **Peter**)   Me too.

Peter   I'm sorry.

Alana   Don't be sorry. Why are you sorry?

Peter   Because . . . Oh shit, I thought . . . I was going to, you know, kiss you tonight. But I was too nervous. And now I'm too drunk and you'll think I'm just kissing you because I'm drunk.

Alana kisses **Peter** *full on the lips. They descend into a long snog.* **Peter** *bolts and vomits on the other side of the bed.*

Alana   I have to ask you something.

Peter (*spitting*)   Yeah?

Alana   Do you want sex or don't you?

Peter   What, now?

Alana   No, I mean, just, in general.

Peter   Um, I don't know, yes?

Alana   Ok.

Peter   Do you?

Alana   Yeah. At some point.

Peter   Cool.

Belches.

Good.

Alana (*to the audience*)   And so we were a couple.

Peter   Does that mean we're going to Prom together?

Alana   Yes, we had Prom at our school. GCSE Prom. It was great actually. I had my hair done specially and bought a really expensive dress and really expensive lingerie because . . .

(*Smirking.*)   Pete booked a room. For the night. Of course we'd have to leave early, but it was exciting, to go to a hotel – all posh – it was all very exciting, all so exciting that I was sick in the lobby. In the toilets in the lobby, not in the lobby itself, not just on the marble or anything, I made it to the toilet. I wasn't drunk. I didn't want to be drunk. Not for this. We had this idea that we'd lose our virginity together. That night. We wanted it to be – American.

They sink down onto the bed.

Alana   And it was all beautiful and I was ready and he was soft and warm and gentle over me and it – it – it was like, hitting a wall.

Ah!

A brick wall.

Peter   Um, it's not going . . . –

Alana (*to* **Peter**)   You're not hard enough.

Peter   – Is that normal? I am hard!

Alana (*to the audience*)   Like punching a grazed knee. Ah!

Peter   Are you alright?

Alana (*to the audience*)   Like scraping . . . the back of your . . . throat . . .

Alana *passes out.* **Peter** *is very still.*

Peter (*beat*)   Lani? Alana!

Peter *shakes her.*

Peter   Can you hear me! Oh fuck fuck fuck fuck fuck – Alana!

Peter *tries to wake her, eventually slapping her on the face to bring her around.* **Alana** *wakes up seizing, her whole body convulsing and shaking.* **Peter** *just holds her, terrified. Eventually she breaks out of it and breathes in big gulps of air, getting her bearings. They lock eyes.*

Peter   What was that what happened what's wrong.

Alana *can't speak.*

Peter   I'm sorry, I'm sorry, I'm so so sorry, I'm sorry / I'm sorry I'm sorry I'm sorry I'm sorry . . .

Alana   I'm sorry I'm sorry I'm sorry I'm sorry I'm sorry . . .

Eventually **Alana** *faces the audience.*

Alana (*to the audience*)   We didn't talk about it. And we both promised not to tell. We just . . . avoided it. Just kept on doing, other things. Sexy things. Just never inside. It was fine. It was nice.

(*To* **Peter**.) I don't know how you can bear to lick it.

Peter   I don't know how you can bear to suck it.

Alana *shrugs, 'fair point'.*

I'm glad you do.

Alana (*to the audience*)   He was much more relaxed after that, funnily enough, more confident. Maybe he thought it was his big dick that did it.

GCSEs came and went and I did alright. And then I was in 6th Form. And everything was so different, I didn't have to wear a tie – Pete still had to – and I could wear jewellery – within reason – and I basically didn't have to do PE anymore. Well, I did, but I didn't really. Every Wednesday the last two periods were set aside for exercise and there was this gym in town we were allowed to use but it wasn't supervised and my mum didn't get home until way after I did, so we'd go to my house and fool around. It was aerobic! Pete had one of these – bionic penises. That could just keep going and going and I don't mean for ages at a time, I mean again and again. It wouldn't be too long after we'd finished that he'd:

Peter *kisses her neck, strokes her.*

Alana (*to* **Peter**)   Give me a second.

Peter   Alright.

He flops away.

Alana   Oh not like that. Come here.

They spoon together. **Alana** *giggles.*

Peter   What?

Alana   Your willy.

Peter   What?

Alana   I can feel it. Pressing.

Peter   Well what do you expect?

Alana   It's not normal.

Peter   It's my gift!

Alana   High metabolism is a gift.

Peter   Hey, I've not got much going for me but I've got this.

Alana   Shut up you're perfect.

She kisses him. They snuggle closer. She squirms.

Alana   It's in my back though.

Peter   Ugh, fine, hold on.

He adjusts himself.

Alana   Argh! No!

Peter   What?

Alana   I don't want your ball sweat on my back!

Peter   Ok, look, I'll push it down . . .

He does so.

Peter   There. Better?

Alana   Yeah. It's in my bum though.

Peter   Not in.

Alana   Between.

Peter   It's nice. Isn't it?

Alana   I guess.

Peter   It, could go in. If you wanted it to.

Alana   What?

Peter   I mean, I'm just saying.

Alana   You want –

Peter   It's just a possibility that's all I'm saying.

Alana   I don't think I – could.

Peter   Why not? Shit goes in and out every day.

Alana   Pete!

Peter   It's true!

Alana   Only out!

Peter   Well, same thing isn't it.

Alana   This is disgusting.

Peter   Well, I'm just saying. Forget about it if you like.

Alana (*beat*)   We could . . .

Peter   What?

Alana   See.

Peter   . . . Yeah?

Alana *shrugs.*

Peter   Oh my god really?

Alana   . . . Yeah.

Peter   Amazing.

Alana   Just . . . put it . . . against it . . .

Peter   Ok. There?

Alana   Yeah –?

Peter   I think that's it. Yeah. What now?

Alana   Um, just – I don't know.

Peter   I'll just . . .

Alana   Don't push.

Peter   No I'll just, let it, press . . . It's nice.

Alana   Yeah?

Peter   Yeah.

Peter *spits on her (between her cheeks).*

Alana   What are you doing!

Peter   I saw it – it'll help.

Alana   I don't like it!

Peter   Sorry, do you want / some –

Alana   No!

Peter   – . . . lube?

Alana   . . . No.

Peter   Ok.

They wait in silence. **Alana**'*s eyes widen.*

Alana   Oh.

Peter   Was that –?

Alana   See.

Peter   What that –?

Alana   Yeah.

Peter   Was it –?

Alana   Yeah.

Peter   Ok?

Alana   . . . Yeah.

Peter   Ok.

They wait again.

Alana   Ooooh . . .

Peter   Are you –?

Alana   No I'm fine.

Another pause.

Alana   You're pushing!

Peter   I am not!

Alana   Well, do then.

Peter   Push?

Alana   Yeah.

Peter   Really?

Alana   Yeah.

He pushes. **Alana** *softly groans.*

Peter   Amazing . . .

Alana   Yeah.

Peter   Do we need / condoms or . . .?

Alana   Shh.

Peter   Is it –?

Alana   Just, go.

Peter   Alright.

He begins to move his hips back and forth.

Alana   Oh my god.

Peter   Oh my god. Are you –?

Alana   It's fine.

Peter   Ok just –

Alana   Don't, shh . . .

Peter   But tell me –

Alana   What!

Peter   If I should stop.

Alana   Don't stop!

Peter   Yeah ok. Amazing.

*They continue to move together. They are both enjoying this. They moan
a little.*

Peter   Oh my god. Oh my god.

Alana   Yes.

Peter   Oh my god.

Alana   Thank god.

Peter   Oh – oh my – oh –

Alana   Are you coming?

Peter   Uh – oh – y-y-yes –

Alana   Oh my god.

Peter   Should I not?

Alana   No. Go on.

Peter   Inside?

Alana   Yes yes.

Peter   Oh my god I love you.

Alana   I love you too!

Peter   This is amazing. I'm going to come!

Alana   Come inside me! I want it inside me!

Peter   Here it comes!

He comes. They groan together.

Mother (*calling*)   Alana come down here!

Alana   Shit!

She pulls herself away from him.

Stay here!

Peter *hides under the covers.* **Alana** *goes to her mother.*

Alana   You're home.

Mother   I heard everything.

Alana   Everything everything?

Mother   Everything.

Alana   Why are you home?

Mother   Bomb scare.

Alana   Ah.

Beat.

I'm sorry.

Silence.

Mother   Wait here.

Mother *leaves.* **Alana** *looks to the audience pleadingly.* **Mother** *returns
with a packet of Microgynon.*

Mother   These are mine. We'll get you your own prescription but in the
meantime – and I hope you used a condom?

Alana   But / we . . .

Mother   But what. You don't want to get pregnant do you.

Alana   . . . No.

Mother   So this weekend we're getting you pills and condoms and then that's the end of it.

Alana   Thank you.

Mother   Well. Yes. You are . . .

Mother *awkwardly dismisses her.*

Alana (*to the audience*)   I couldn't tell her what happened. What was happening. That I definitely wouldn't get pregnant.

We both got into Uni. Me and Pete. I went to Exeter. Pete went to Oxford . . . Brookes. He lost weight and I gained it. And the distance sucked but for the first time I was really, excited. I had a new page, you know, a clean slate. I could be, who I wanted to be. Who I was. And for the first time, I actually chose my friends.

Sally   I can only come from oral sex. I'm serious, I don't think I even have a g-spot, I think it *is* a myth. Or you know like those people born with a hole in their heart? That's like me and my cunt.

Beat.

Wait . . .

Alana (*to the audience*)   Sally. I loved her. Still do. She was studying Art and Philosophy. She was really cool.

Sally (*into her phone*)   Note: Hole in heart, hole in cunt. G-spot? Bullets? Possibly rats, with pierced ears.

Alana   And she had a thing for taxidermy.

Johnny   That would make a great short.

Alana   Johnny. Film Studies.

Sally   I can't wait to move out of halls into some shithole so I can stop buying mice and start laying traps myself.

Johnny   I promise, when we live together, it'll be in the shittest hole we can find.

Sally (*teasing*)   Not everyone likes their holes filled with shit.

Johnny (*playing*)   Homophobe.

Sally (*playing*)   Piss off.

Alana (*to the audience*)   I was doing Geography and French with a module in Philosophy which is how I met Sally, and then Johnny. Pretty obvious I was there for The Experience. But it was an experience and these two, they . . . They were the best friends I've ever had.

Sally   But you must have an opinion.

Johnny   How am I supposed to know? I'm not interested am I.

Sally   But you're a queer.

Johnny   Which means I like queers. I can tell you if your brother looks good. PS he does, enough to eat, and anyway 'A Queer'? Who says 'A / Queer' anymore?

Sally   But you're meant / to . . .

Johnny   If you asked a hetero if he thinks his mate looks good he'll say the same thing, I don't care how progressive you are.

Sally   But girls tell each other how they look all the time.

Johnny   Yeah that's a girl thing.

Alana   I guess if you've never been with a woman / how can you . . .

Johnny   'Course I have!

Sally   Who!

Johnny   Two actually.

Sally   Who!

Johnny   My neighbour. And my cousin.

Sally *and* **Alana** *laugh.*

Johnny   I was confused. And I'm assuming neither of you have done it with the same sex.

Sally   No. I've been so boring, but I intend to fix that by the end of first year. I have a list: I have never slept with a girl, a black man, an Asian man, any non-white basically. I've never had a threesome, or fucked anyone shorter than me, circumcised or with nipple piercings.

(*To* **Alana**.) Have you?

Alana   None of the above.

Johnny   Or buttsex.

Sally   Or buttsex.

Alana   / I've had . . .

Johnny   I'm circumcised.

Alana   Really?

Johnny   Oh yeah.

Sally   Are you American?

Johnny   What?

Sally   Well you're not Jewish are you.

Alana   Could be Muslim.

Johnny (*very camp*)   Oh yes darling, Allah and all that jazz, I love it it's a scream.

Alana (*laughing despite herself*)   Johnny . . .!

Sally   Well why are you circumcised then?

Johnny   It's not that unusual.

Alana   It is a bit.

Sally   Are your parents neat freaks?

Johnny   No, in fact it had nothing to do with them – what does that even mean? – I had it done.

Alana   What!

Sally   Why!

Alana   When!

Johnny   This one crazy summer, when I was backpacking, and I went to all these festivals – all over the world it was so fantastic – and I just didn't wash.

Sally *retches.*

Alana   Johnny . . .

Johnny   You cannot shame me. I've learned my lesson and I am not that person anymore.

Alana   So what, did it get – infected?

Johnny   More like invaded. Totally taken over, pillaged by tiny little mucus-making fungi and, other things.

Sally *and* **Alana** *scream and giggle with gross-glee.*

Johnny   So I said 'Ok, Doc, do your worst'.

Sally   Did it hurt?

Johnny   What do you think.

Alana   And now you're – ?

Johnny   As a whistle.

Alana   What's it like?

Johnny   It's fine.

Sally   Is it less sensitive?

Johnny   It was more, at first. But now I guess – I don't know. Maybe.

Alana   I've never even seen one.

Sally   Yes you have . . .

Alana   No.

Sally   What about porn?

Johnny   Woah. Neither of you have had a trimmed cock?

Sally *and* **Alana** *shake their heads.*

Johnny (*getting up onto the bed*)   The things I do for love.

Sally   Steady on!

Johnny   Just a poke about.

Sally   I don't want a poke from a fag!

Johnny   I meant you, you bint! What, don't you want a look?

Sally   At your dong?

Johnny   Purely research. Don't want you two out of the loop.

Sally   Yes please!

Johnny   Well then be gentle. But. You did call me a fag which is way offensive so Lani gets first go.

Alana (*to the audience*)   They were the best years of my life.

Johnny *has now undone his trousers and* **Sally** *screams with joy.* **Peter** *and* **Alana** *are on the phone to each other. While* **Peter** *actually masturbates,* **Alana** *just talks dirty.*

Peter   What are you wearing?

Alana   Just my panties.

Peter   Which panties?

Alana   The purple ones with the dots.

Peter   Ooh my favourites. Are they clean?

Alana   No . . .

Peter   What?

Alana   I mean, no because they're wet. Because you made me wet. / Talking . . .

Peter   Oh. Yeah that's nice. Are you touching yourself?

Alana   Oh yeah.

Peter   Do you want a hand?

Alana   I've got a hand I need a dick.

Peter   I think I've got what you need right here . . .

Alana   Ooh is it a big one?

Peter   How about you see how big you can get it.

Alana   Mm ish sho big in ma mouf, is tu big.

Peter   Yeah, suck it while I rub you.

Alana   Uh I like tasting it.

Peter   Your tongue feels good.

Alana   I'm getting it deeper and deeper.

Peter   I'm getting stiffer and stiffer.

Alana   I'm practically choking on it.

Peter   You're so wet.

Alana   I'm so so wet.

Peter   I'm burying my face in you.

Alana   How does that work?

Peter (*beat*)   I've changed position.

Alana   Oh ok.

Peter   You're lying on the bed.

Alana   I'm lying on the bed.

Peter   You're trembling under my face.

Alana   I can't help it it feels so good.

Peter   I'm jacking off while I eat you out.

Alana   I love it when you wank to me.

Peter   I can't help myself, I just thrust myself into you!

Alana   Ooooh!

Peter   And I'm thrusting and I'm pummelling.

Alana   Thrust me! Pummel me! You big cock fucker!

Peter   And I shove my thumb into your ass!

Alana   Shove your – what?

Peter   Am I breaking up?

Alana   Say that again?

Peter   Into – your – ass.

Alana   So what are you fucking?

Peter   What?

Alana   Are you putting your thumb in there with your dick or are you – what what are you saying?

Peter   What are you saying?

Alana   Where is your dick?

Peter   In your gash!

Beat.

What?

Alana   But that's not . . .

Peter   I know. We're pretending though, aren't we.

Alana   Yeah but . . .

Peter   I mean my thumb isn't actually in your arse right now is it / –

Alana   Yeah but . . .

Peter   – you're not actually choking / on my . . .

Alana   But you know I don't like it!

Beat.

How am I meant to get off if you're talking about – that.

Peter (*sighing*)   So, what, I can't even hope now?

Alana   What?

Peter   Hello!

Alana   I can hear you I just . . . what are you talking about?

Peter   Are we ever going to have sex, Alana?

Alana *is silent.*

Peter   Because I don't know about you but it's a bit weird being the only guy here who's a virgin. Technically. When he's been with his girlfriend for three years. It's not normal is it.

Beat.

We need to – figure this out. Because, you know, I've been patient. Haven't I.

Alana   You've – we've – We have fun though, right? What we / do –?

Peter   Of course we have fun.

Alana   Are you not – is it not enough anymore?

Peter   It's . . . I . . . look, I love you.

Beat.

I met someone last night.

Beat.

I wasn't going to tell you, because nothing happened. Because I love you. So much. But I – was tempted. Because – you know. And it's not every day someone comes up to me . . .
(*Sighing.*) I don't know what to do. I love you. I mean am I being / unfair?

Alana (*lying*)   I fingered myself.

Peter   You what?

Alana   The other day. I wasn't going to tell you. It was going to be a surprise. But I think I'm – ready.

Peter   Really?

Alana   Yeah. I don't want to lose you.

Peter   I don't want to lose you either.

Alana   I love you.

Peter   I love you too.

Alana (*to the audience*)   I took a train that night.

(*To* **Peter**.)   Slowly slowly slowly . . .

Peter   Shhh . . .

Alana   Sorry. Sorry.

Peter   Is that –?

Alana   Umm, it's not . . .

Alana *takes very deep breaths.* **Peter** *pushes into her and* **Alana** *can't help but scream.*

Peter   Lani!

Alana   Don't –! Warn / me first!

Peter   My housemates will hear!

Alana   It hurts!

Peter   I know it hurts! I'm sorry it hurts! What do you want me to do!

Alana   Ok, actually, just go for it. Notnow! Just, when I say, ok, you just thrust it in, like a plaster, just do it, quickly. When I say.

Peter   Alright . . .

Alana   Ready?

Peter   Yes.

Beat.

Are you?

Alana   In a minute.

Peter *sighs and shifts.*

Just give me a minute!

Peter   I'm giving you a minute!

Alana   I'm giving you my virginity!

Peter   Don't act like this is some special fucking thing because it's not! Everyone does it, Lani! Everyone gets over it! You're not fucking special!

Alana (*beat*)   Can't your housemates hear you.

Peter   Ready?

Alana   No.

Peter   One . . .

Alana   Pete!

Peter   I'm going to lose it . . .

Alana   Ok. One . . . two, three.

Peter *thrusts up into her and she screams again.*

Peter   Shh!

Alana   Get out get out get out get out get out get out.

Peter *pulls out and off to the side.*

Alana   I'm not frigid. You know I'm not. I do / really want . . .

Peter   Just relax. Just . . . just sleep.

Alana (*to the audience*)   We somehow managed the whole night without touching. Not once. He had lectures in the morning. I woke up and he'd already gone. When I got home I had an email waiting for me:

Peter   Alana, I have a few things I need to say to you. First I'm really sorry about what happened, I didn't mean to snap at you, I know it was difficult for both of us but I did and I'm sorry, I just panicked. I really love you and I always have but I think we should probably split up. I still love you that's nothing to do with it, but I feel like I've grown up with you and really learned so much from you and now I need to do that on my own a bit because we're sort of staying still if you know what I mean. I would never want to hurt you, which is why this whole thing is so hard, and love shouldn't be this hard you know? I hope you don't hate me for doing this online, I knew if I did it over Skype or in person I would screw it up. I know that's not good enough. I still love you as I love all my friends and I want us to be friends because I think you're great and I would never want to lose such a great friend, but I hope you understand why I want to do this and I hope you'll respect that. I'm really really sorry, Lani.

Desperate, she darts up to her knees, legs apart. She rummages around and puts her hand up under herself. She struggles getting her hand in place. She becomes still, eyes wide. She closes them, breathing deeply, pushing the air out through puckered lips. She screws up her eyes, furrowing her brow, straining. She gasps and a jolt goes through her. She shakes her head again, inhales, winces, eventually must cry out, pulling her hand out. She hangs her head, shoulders tense, shaking from clenched muscles. She flings her head back, defeated. She wipes her eyes.

Alana   The problem was me. Obviously. But more than that, what I mean is I had too much control, I was never going to do it when I could just say no. I needed to just do it.

I thought about walking through parks alone at night, hanging around dark alleys . . . waiting for someone who wouldn't take no for an answer. Then I had a better idea.

Club music. **Alana** *dances.*

Alana   I hate clubs. The music – not only is it just bad, it's too loud. How are you meant to say anything, hold a conversation, how are you meant to get to know anybody? But then, I guess, that's the idea.

Mark *dances.*

Alana   For example, we didn't have to chat for me to know: he'd do.

Mark *and* **Alana** *make out outside the club. They grope each other. She digs her hand into his trousers. He laughs. His laughs turn into a moan and then:*

Mark   Woah, wait, wait!

He ejaculates. Awkward silence.

Don't worry. I'll be better at my place.

Alana (*to the audience*)   We managed to make it to his bedroom without incident and I even got him mostly undressed, but . . .

Mark *has fallen asleep. He snores.* **Alana** *sighs.* **Alana** *takes out her phone and calls* **Johnny**, *gets his answerphone:*

Johnny   This is Johnny, I can't come to the phone right now, unlucky! Leave a message if you like, but I don't check them, so BBM me if you really care.

Alana *tries calling* **Sally** *and gets through:*

Sally (*whispering*)   Hi what's up?

Alana (*whispering*)   Why are you whispering?

Sally (*whispering*)   Why are you whispering?

Alana (*whispering, looking at* **Mark**)   Because . . . you are.

Sally (*whispering*)   I'm with someone.

Alana (*whispering*)   Oh.

Sally (*whispering*)   So I can't be long. I'm in his en-suite picking toilet paper off my flaps.

Alana (*whispering*)   What?

Sally (*whispering*)   Don't you get that?

Alana (*whispering*)   No.

Sally (*whispering*)   I do. I thought everyone did. Listen was there something specific?

Alana (*whispering*)   Uh . . . no, just a chat.

Sally (*whispering*)   You alright?

Alana (*whispering*)   Yeah of course yeah. I'll leave you to it.

Sally (*whispering*)   Ok great thanks, see you tomorrow.

Alana (*whispering*)   See you tomorrow.

Sally (*whispering*)   Ooh ooh Lani Lani Lani!

Alana (*whispering*)   What?

Sally (*whispering*)   He's Mexican!

Alana (*whispering*)   Who?

Sally (*whispering*)   My conquest!

Alana (*whispering*)   Oh great, good, another box ticked.

Sally (*whispering*)   Yeah and with the Chinese guy last week I feel much better about myself. Chinese? Or Korean?

Alana (*whispering*)   You fucked him!

Sally (*whispering*)   I'll check his Facebook page . . . Sayonara!

Sally *hangs up.* **Alana** *shoves* **Mark** *so he rolls off the bed.*

Doctor   Hello, sorry about the wait, one of our nurses is off sick and we're a little behind, so –

(*Joking voice.*) – What are you in for?

The **Doctor** *gives a little laugh.*

Alana   Well, what I want to know is, I want to know if someone could just medically, surgically even, remove my virginity? Just put me under, break me in.

Doctor   O-kaaay, let's see, maybe. Why do you want to know that?

Alana   I can't do it.

Doctor   What's the problem?

Alana   Me, obviously.

Doctor   I'm sure there's nothing wrong with you, what I mean is, what's causing the trouble?

Alana   No there is. I can't even get close.

Doctor   You know lots of girls have their first experiences later on in life . . .

Alana   No I've had boyfriends, I've done things, I just . . . can't. I just can't. I don't know why, I don't know what the problem is, I don't know what's wrong with me or what I should do differently. Is there an operation so I can just get it over with?

Doctor   Are you talking about your hymen?

Alana   If that's what will do it.

Doctor (*beat*)   I'm going to ask you a few questions if that's alright? They might be a bit embarrassing.

Alana   Alright.

Doctor   Are you sure you're using the right hole?

Alana   Yes.

Doctor   Do you wash thoroughly?

Alana   Yes.

Doctor   Do you look at yourself, often?

Alana   I have done.

Doctor   What about recently?

Alana   A bit.

Doctor   Do you masturbate?

Alana   Not really. Never . . . [inside]

Doctor   Ok, and so you've tried with partners, but what about yourself, on your own?

Alana   Yes.

Doctor   And what does it feel like? When you've tried.

Alana   Like . . . like there's something in the way? And it stings. Like it's raw, like there's no skin, just . . . it really hurts.

Doctor   Ok. It's probably vaginismus.

Alana   Oh. What?

Doctor   I'd like to examine you, if you don't mind?

Alana *is unsure.*

Doctor   I don't have to go inside if you don't want me to, but it would be good, just to do.

Alana *takes a deep breath and lies down on the bed. The* **Doctor** *puts on gloves.*

Doctor   Thanks, that's great. So vaginismus is a psychosexual problem, it's when the muscles in the walls of your vagina spasm uncontrollably and cause a lot of pain and we happen to have a very good department for it here, so you're in luck. Plenty of people get over it. Now it may not be that, but it sounds a lot like it so I'd just like to eliminate the possibilities there's something physical causing you trouble, ok? Just spread your legs for me and move your feet up towards your bottom ok? Just so you're comfortable. Great . . .

The **Doctor** *examines her.*

Doctor   Great . . . Just a little pressure now . . .

Alana *winces.*

Doctor   That's it. You're doing very well, this is great, really useful. Ok. Now I'd like to go inside just a little if you'll let me?

Alana *is silent.*

Doctor   Is that alright?

Alana *shakes her head.*

Doctor   Ok that's fine not a problem, not a problem at all.

The **Doctor** *stands up and takes off her gloves.*

Doctor   You can put your pants on now.

Alana *does so.*

Doctor   Hard to relax, isn't it.

Alana *nods.*

Doctor   So. A couple things, everything looks fine, very normal, just a few things that might be causing some problems nothing major. Ok, so everyone has a little bridge of skin at the bottom of the opening of their vagina, and that's usually pretty elastic but in your case it's quite tight, that's what that slight pressure was, just me testing its give, and there wasn't much there I'm sure you felt it. And that will probably improve with use but as you're not using it, it's not going to get any more flexible. And that's the first thing I'd suggest, is just to start exploring that for yourself and getting used to putting pressure on that part of you – go home and have a good look in the mirror, do you have a hand-held mirror? Just place it on the floor beneath you and have a good rummage, ok? Everyone's different and you're perfectly normal but that's your little difference, ok? Vaginismus is, unfortunately, self-affirming, so if you had some pain the first time you interacted with your vagina in that way the body remembers and the next time you try it's expecting that pain so it's a bit worse and sometimes the spiral just gets a little out of control and things end up being very difficult. It's nothing to do with you, you're fine. It's not in your control, do you understand? Am I being clear?

Alana *nods and can't help but start to cry. The* **Doctor** *produces some tissues.*

Doctor   Aw sweetheart that's fine, you cry if you want to, it's all a bit much, isn't it. Me rabbiting on at you like that, it's a bit much, hm? Have a good cry, that's good now. Are you going to be alright?

Alana *nods.*

Do you want to speak to someone? A counsellor?

Alana   I just want to fix it.

Doctor   Ok. That can happen. It will be very straightforward, I promise.

Alana   Thank you.

Doctor   No thank you. That was very brave of you to do, you know that? And you've done very well, no screams huh! I've had screamers! We'll sort you out, ok? Now, there are lots of options available to you. I don't think there's surgery that will help, and I'd much rather get you straightened out holistically anyway, and remember, almost everyone gets over this with time and a little work. So that's what I'd like to do. Like I said there's a great psychosexual department here and what I'd like to do is book you an appointment to meet one of the psychiatrists there, just an introduction, just to get an initial assessment, and then we can go from there. There's a ten step treatment plan you can go into, which includes counselling and graduated vaginal insertions – those are with little dildos made from a very strong glass of varying widths, and you work your way up. As well as these there's exercises you do with your assigned physician, as well as Kegel exercises you can do on your own at home, and of course no one's expecting you to accomplish this over night . . .

Alana's *eyes have glazed over a little.* **Doctor** *has moved away.*

Alana (*to the audience, crying*)   She was so fucking lovely.
(*Composing herself.*) I don't know why I cried.
(*Calming down.*) I don't know why I didn't go back.

Alana *lashes out, punching the bed in frustration.*

I'm sorry. Sorry. I just – I really hate myself because I should have told her – said something like 'I'm sorry for crying, it's just no one else has spoken to me like that before, has cared so much about me, has been so tender when touching me and I know it's not professional but could I have a little cuddle because I feel a bit like you're my mum right now'. I should have gone back and done whatever she told me to do, and stuck with it, even if it was hard and . . . scary. But I was feeling – it was all a bit – and I just went home. Had a shower. Watched iPlayer. A documentary I think. Fell asleep. Woke up. Watched the rest, the bits I missed, and that's when Johnny and Sally:

Sally   Can we come iii-in?

Alana   Yeah hi.

Sally   Hi.

Johnny   Hi.

Alana   Hi(?) What's up?

Sally   We want to talk to you.

Alana   . . . Ok(?)

Sally (*beat*)   Are you alright?

Alana   Yeah(?)

Sally   Are you sure?

Alana   Yeah I'm fine, why?

Sally   Well it's just – we thought – . . . We know.

Alana (*horror*)   What.

Johnny   I saw you. Coming out the doctor's. Red face and everything, so . . .

Alana   I didn't see you where were you.

Johnny   Across the street.

Sally   In the bushes.

Johnny   Figured it was something private.

Sally   So what's going on? You can tell us.

Johnny   We're here for you.

Sally   She knows we're here for her.

Johnny   Well she knows she can tell us too!

Sally   Obviously she doesn't or she would have already.

Johnny (*to* **Alana**)   Don't listen to her. Do what you want. Tell us, or tell us to fuck off. But we are here.

Alana (*to the audience*)   They were my best friends. She had a hole in her G-spot, she'd understand. I could talk to Johnny about the buttsex! This was the perfect opportunity! This was my chance!

(*To* **Johnny** *and* **Sally**.) I've – I've got . . . I've got a yeast infection.

Johnny *tries to stifle a laugh.* **Sally** *shoots him a look.*

Sally   Babe, that's nothing to cry about.

Alana   I know it's just, it was just a shock. I'm very clean.

Sally   I know you are.

Johnny   You are.

Sally   Sometimes that's what does it though. Do you use scented stuff? That can give you trouble.

Alana   Just Dove.

Sally (*hugging her*)   Oh Honey, it's so unfair.

Johnny *joins the hug.*

Alana (*to the audience*)   I decided, fuck it. Forget it. You know? Forget it. This is how it's going to be. From here on out. I spent the next two years single. I lived like a nun with no god. Or at least, a god I hated. Graduated with a First. Left uni. Got a job. Stayed in touch with Sally and Johnny, worked my arse off and finally got my own flat. A really nice place actually. With a little balcony and a fireplace and a Sometimes Double.

All to myself.

Just had to get the last of my stuff from my mum's place.

Alana *takes out her phone and taps it.*

Mother (*calling*)   You could help me you know.

Alana   I'm just finishing this email.

Mother (*calling*)   Can it wait?

Alana   It's to Sally.

Mother (*calling*)   How is she?

Alana   Inviting me to her solo show.

Mother (*calling*)   You remember Jess.

Alana   Yes.

Mother (*calling*)   She's pregnant.

Alana (*beat*)   Really.

Mother (*calling*)   You can tell.

Alana   Well good for her.

Mother (*calling*)   How do you know it's good news?

Alana (*irritated*)   I don't, Mum, I don't know, but I also don't assume the worst, I have a positive attitude.

Mother (*calling*)   I'm just saying! I'm just making conversation!

Alana (*to the audience*)   As if she'd ever done that before. I'd asked her to put everything in a box in advance, there wasn't much, it shouldn't have taken this long. In and out, job done. Should have known that was never my luck.

Alana's *phone rings, she answers it.*

Hello?

(*To the audience.*) Telephone voice.

(*To the caller again.*) Yes it is.

Yes I just moved.

Yes actually I'm glad you called, that's the right address but I have asked you to stop sending them.

Yes I know but I don't have them.

Actually I have asked my GP and I . . .

Yes Doctor Simmons.

Checks if her mother is in earshot.

It should be on my file why I'm not having them.

Can you not just check the file please?

No I –

Calls.

Mum?

Beat.

(*Hushed.*) I have vaginismus.

Yes, so I can't . . .

No, never.

Yes so it's very unlikely.

Well I couldn't have the smear anyway could I!

(*Lowering her voice.*) It just not possible for me.

Ok thank you. Thank you.

She lets out a frustrated sigh.

Mother (*calling*)   Alana?

Alana   Yes, Mum.

Mother (*calling*)   Um – where's the show?

Alana   Shoreditch.

Mother (*calling*)   When is it?

Alana   You wouldn't like it.

Mother (*entering with a box*)   I might.

Alana   You wouldn't.

(*Taking the box.*) Thanks.

Mother (*keeping hold of the box*)   Have you been raped?

Alana   What? No.

Mother   Have you?

Alana   No!

Mother   You promise me?

Alana   I promise I have not been raped! Why are / you asking . . .?

Mother   Then what's happened to you?

Alana   Nothing's happened! I don't know what you're / on about!

Mother   I know what vaginismus is.

Stunned silence.

It's when you're raped or molested and you're traumatized and / you can't . . .

Alana   That's not, that's not what it is.

Mother   What is it then?

Alana   It's nothing. It's fine, everything's fine.

Mother   Who were you talking to.

Alana   None of your business and I can't / believe you were listening!

Mother (*breaking*)   Of course it's my bloody business you're my bloody daughter!

Pause.

Tell me what it is. Please.

Alana   It's just something I had, and it's not a problem now.

Mother   You still have it?

Alana   No.

Mother   You said you did, on the phone.

Alana   I misspoke.

Mother (*beat*)   Fine.

Awkward silence.

Mother *hugs* **Alana**, *patting her on the back.*

Alana (*to the audience, still hugging*)   It was a man hug. Pat on the back and everything. And it hit me. She was shit at this. Never was any good at this stuff. And that's not her fault.
It's just the way she is.

I felt so sad just then, for a second, for her.

Mother   Was it my fault?

Alana   No.

Mother   And you're ok now?

Alana   Yes.

(*To the audience.*) I think she knew I was lying. Believed me anyway. I think she really needed to. So did I.

Johnny   This is fantastic! It's glorious isn't it! So edgy!

Sally   What are you wearing?

Johnny   Too much?

Sally   I thought you were going to wear my dress.

Johnny   I thought we were joking.

Sally   I wasn't.

Johnny   You don't want a bad cliché walking around your show.

Sally   Yes I do. What's the point in having gay friends if no one knows you have them.

Johnny   Why am I your friend?

Sally   Go home and change, please. Please? For me?

Johnny   It's not your wedding!

Sally   I don't believe in weddings, I believe they're an archaic patriarchal trap, so this might as well be. It might be the / closest I come to one.

Johnny   Oh my god fine fine fine fine fine.

(*Exiting.*) I'm a person. I'm a person!

Sally *faces* **Alana** *and points to her own head, questioning.*

Alana (*reassuring*)   The show's great, Sally . . .

Sally   Look while we have a sec, I want to say something to you, ok? What I want to say is that this is my night, yeah?

Alana   Yeah(?)

Sally   But you should think about it as yours. Lani. Now's your time. I can feel it. You know I feel these things. It's been a long time since Pete and you – and Pete was a nice guy but honestly he wasn't that nice and you need to let him go, he's not worth this, you need to get fucked. Basically. I'm not talking drinking I'm talking with a penis in your vagina, that's just what you need to do now. It'll launch you over that hurdle, get you back on the horse you need to ride. You know?

Alana   Sally / I . . .

Sally   You are sexy! You are so sexy!

Alana   I'm / . . .

Sally   And not in a conventional way, sure, and maybe that's why some people don't see it but I see it, I see your sexiness, you need to see your sexiness and run with it! Just have sex with someone, anyone, anyone here, pick anyone. Except for the guy with the grey bow tie because that's Morgan Twist and he owns a gallery. But anyone else. And just let them ram you, it's that simple. Ok? Just do it. Don't be scared. It's easy. There he is I've got to go.

Alana *is left shocked, frustrated, a little angry, and amused.*

Alana (*to the audience*)   I mean, I love her, but sometimes . . .

Alana *catches* **Gerry** *looking her up and down. He looks away. She shares her disapproval with the audience. He looks at her directly. She realizes, looks back at him. He smiles. She questions him with a turn of her head.*

Gerry   What do you think?

Alana   About what?

(*To the audience.*) Had he heard?

Gerry   The 'Art'?

Alana   I like it.

Gerry   You do.

Alana   Yes.

Gerry   You don't think it's sensationalist, vacuous and immature?

Alana   No.

Gerry   What do you think it is?

Alana   My friend's expression / of her talent –

Gerry   Ah.

Alana   – and creativity.

Gerry   And sexuality.

Alana   Excuse me?

Gerry   Obviously.

Alana (*to the audience*)   He had heard.

Gerry   Isn't it?

Alana   No.

Gerry   You don't think so?

Alana   Explain to me how a dead rabbit and some bashed-up butterflies are expressions of my best friend's sexuality.

Gerry   Your best friend is it? Well, it's about transformation yes? From a girl into a woman. The imagery is relatively plain. The Bashed-Up Butterflies have wings like labia, don't they, like thighs. And their abdomens obviously look like cunts. You're not offended are you good. The rabbit is the chase, the panting, the exhaustion, running down its hole. And with its arms out, like so, there are clear references to religious ecstasy, pain and pleasure, rapture, you must know what I mean. And then there's the big wooden spike piercing through its soft, furry underside.

Beat.

I'm a curator.

Alana   I'm frigid.

Gerry (*beat*)   I'm sorry?

Alana   My cunt doesn't work. It's broken. I've never had sex and I never will. So actually, no, I don't know what you mean. At all. So.

Gerry (*presenting his hand for her to shake*)   I'm Gerry.

Alana   Hi Gary.

Gerry   Gerry.

Alana   Jerry?

Gerry   Geh-ree. It's Welsh.

Alana   Ah.

Gerry   I'm not.

Alana   Ok.

Gerry   Do you have a name?

Alana   Alana.

Gerry   Alana I'm so sorry. I've been so rude to you. Let me make it up to you. There's a restaurant I know just around the corner. Let me buy you dinner.

Alana (*to the audience, shrugging*)   Free dinner.

*The **Waitress** brings olives for them and they sit.*

Gerry   Now I don't want you telling anybody about this place, any of the New Age Vintage Plaid Ironic Dickheads from back there. They'll ruin it.

Alana   What's around your neck?

Gerry   India. Here, have one.

Takes one out of his pocket and gives it to her.

I give them to people who are, significant. And when I run out I know it's time to go back. You don't have to believe in it or anything, just take it.

Alana   What is it?

Gerry   It's Amitabh. There are four Buddhas, each pointing to a different pole, and he's pointing to the west pole.

Alana   There is no west pole.

Gerry   No, the western hemisphere, the western, the west.

Alana *smirks.*

Gerry   They sell them outside this cave I go to in Ajanta. Inside is this enormous carving of Amitabh. Enormous. You have to climb this mountain to get there, it's a small mountain but it's not a hill. Couldn't jog up there, unless you're a fell runner like my son – runs up the bloody things, it's ridiculous, he's going to kill himself. Anyway you don't run but when you get almost to the top there's this opening – someone's carved into the rock with their hands – and you walk in and it's pitch black and you have to trust . . . well there's nothing to trust, you just have to go forward through this series of rooms all in a straight line. Your eyes adjust. There are the most beautiful carvings, ornamentation, bats. And the light from behind you starts to get fainter but your eyes adjust and eventually you see – his toe. That's it. His toe, as tall as you are and when you realize what you're looking at you look up, instinctively you look up and there, it, is. Towering above you. Carved out of the rock. Wonderful. I always get out, fall to the floor, and sob.

Alana   Wow.

Gerry   It is. Quite wow.

Alana   Are you bullshitting me?

Gerry *laughs and looks at his menu.*

Gerry   I'm starving.

Pause.

If anything goes wrong over there they just make a religion out of it. I think it's very healthy. Born with five legs? Instant deity. You'd be a goddess.

Alana (*to the audience*)   It was cheap, and he was rude and arrogant and a hypocrite and too old for me and full of shit and not good-looking but not bad-looking and yet, I found myself sucking on those olives, very – suggestively. And checking in the windows that I looked good doing it.

She takes an olive, sucks it, looks to the audience as if there's a window and sees the face she's pulling – it makes her stop immediately.

Gerry   Would you like to go to bed with me?

Alana (*beat*)   No.

Gerry *shrugs and looks again at his menu.* **Alana** *furrows her brow, trying to figure him out.*

Alana   I couldn't anyway. I said.

Gerry   How did you break your cunt then?

Alana   I didn't break it, it's just broken.

Gerry   Right. That's remarkable.

Alana   Nope.

Gerry   You don't seem bashful about it.

Alana   Actually no one knows but you.

Gerry   I'm honoured. Have you never had sex?

Alana   I've had sex. Just not, you know.

Gerry   Right. So you've always had this?

Alana *nods.*

Gerry   It's really fascinating. Is it hereditary? Or a deformation?

Alana   No just me being useless.

Gerry   Useless(?)

Alana   Well it's my fault. Muscle spasms. If I could just relax them I could just get over it like everyone else does but no, I'm such a baby –

Gerry *throws an olive pip at* **Alana**'*s face.* **Alana** *is shocked and sort of smiling, but can't get any words out.*

Gerry   Now, don't blink.

Gerry *throws another pip at her face.* **Alana** *can't not blink.*

Gerry   See? Now is that your fault?

Long pause as **Alana** *tries to answer, can't, smiles, bats back emotion, clears her throat and says:*

Alana   Alright then.

Gerry   Hmm?

Alana   I'll go to bed with you.
(*To the audience.*)   And I did. A few times.

Gerry *is giving* **Alana** *cunnilingus.*

Alana (*to* **Gerry**)   Oh, oh, oh, yes, oh, yes, oh yes, yes yes yes, yes yes, uh uh yes yes yes yes / –

Gerry *shifts to glance at his watch.*

Alana   – oh yes, oh yes, oh yeah, oh yeah uh oh that's it, oh yeah, oh yeah, oh oh oh oh yeah yeah yeah yeah yeah yeah / –

Gerry *pulls away.*

Alana   – what? What what's wrong?

Gerry   Ten minutes.

Alana   What?

Gerry   It's always ten minutes in.

Alana   What?

Gerry   Alana.

Alana   What?

Gerry   I've had a lot of lovers.

Alana (*beat*)   Fine.

Gerry   And I know what they sound like when they're faking it.

Alana   I'm not faking.

Gerry   Yes you are.

Alana   No I'm not.

Gerry   Yes you are.

Alana   No I'm not!

Gerry   In fact I don't think you've ever had an orgasm with me.

Alana   I'm sure I have.

Gerry *makes a face, making clear she's just proved his point.*

Alana   I definitely have.

Gerry (*a realization*)   Oh goodness.

Alana   What.

Gerry *covers his mouth.*

Alana   What!

Gerry   You've never had an orgasm.

Alana   Yes I have.

Gerry   No, you haven't.

Alana   Of course I have.

Gerry   What was it like?

Alana   Really . . . really good.

Gerry   Do you masturbate?

Alana   No!

Gerry   I think you should.

Alana   I think you should fuck off!

Gerry   Alana, if we're not equal in this, then, then I'm a very bad man. I'm not – and don't want to be – a bad man. I want us to be equals.

Alana   That's really selfish.

Gerry *can't help but laugh at this.*

Alana   Don't laugh at me.

Gerry   I'm sorry. Could you clarify your point?

Alana   So you can still get off, as in Get Off, guilt free, right? Same difference.

Gerry   Whatever the difference if you're not getting something out of this then I'm not interested. Believe it or not.

Alana   Well it is selfish.

Gerry   If you say / so.

Alana   This is typical, this is so typical – I thought you were different you know! But no, it always has to be this way or that way or this thing and if it's not then you'll all just fuck off!

Gerry   Sorry? I don't / understand.

Alana   It's always up to you! What you want! And I thought you didn't have any of that shit those conditions but it turns out you're just as picky as the rest of them you're just hiding it under this 'concern' for my welfare or whatever and that's patronizing and you're not my dad or something you're not even my boyfriend and why can't things be the way they are! Why aren't I enough! As I am! Why am I not enough!

Pause. **Gerry** *genuinely considers this.*

Gerry   You don't want to come? You're not curious.

Alana   Of course I –

(*Sigh.*) I don't think, it's possible for me, anyway.

Gerry   Why not?

Alana   Don't you have to find the G-spot.

Gerry   No. If you'd masturbated . . .

(*Stops himself.*) I'm sorry. I didn't, approach this, delicately. I felt like a fool, I thought you thought I was a fool and I thought you were doing me a disservice but, I think actually, you've been done the disservice. And this might upset you, and I think maybe I'm close to understanding why, but I'm not comfortable continuing that disservice. I did enough of that when I was your age and an idiot. I'm not saying you're an idiot. But clearly you've slept with some.

Alana   That is true.

He holds his arms open for her to come to him. She rolls her eyes and does, he settles with his arms around her, embracing her from behind – she is not on his lap. He takes her hand and kisses it, then places it between her legs. **Alana** *allows this, but from her expression she clearly doesn't expect much.*

Gerry   I'm not going in.

Alana   Good idea.

Gerry *moves her hand in her crotch with her, pleasuring her. He closes his eyes and becomes very absorbed –* **Alana** *steals a look at his face and it makes her stifle a laugh. She relaxes, smiling, sort of rolling her eyes at the activity. Then she notices something, her expression shifts to acknowledge it: a new feeling. Not necessarily pleasurable, yet. It grows. She tracks its progress. Then a spasm of surprising sensation. Another spasm. Her eyelids flutter, almost closed, as she submits to this rise of feeling. She moves her hips.* **Gerry** *watches her, responding.* **Alana** *nods, eyes closed, little grunts. This all builds. She pushes* **Gerry**'s *hand away, continuing on her own, until she comes quietly in his arms.*

Beat.

Psychiatrist   And that was the only orgasm you'd had?

Alana (*to the audience*)   Yeah. Until that point. Not anymore. After that we – as in right after, the first time . . .

Gerry's *hand is hidden underneath her.*

Alana (*to* **Gerry**)   . . . Are you –?

Gerry *raises his eyebrows and nods.*

Alana   . . . Oh my god.

Gerry   It was very easy. You didn't notice, did you. You're fine, aren't you. It's just there, it's just a finger. You're fine aren't you.

Alana *nods slowly.*

Alana   I'm going to faint.

Gerry   You're not going to faint, no, you're not going to faint – look at me. Are you. You're not going to.

Alana   No. I won't. I'm not going to.

Gerry   No.

They breathe together.

Gerry   You're fine.

Alana   I'm fine.

Gerry   You're fine.

Alana   I'm fine!

Gerry   You're stiff, try to relax.

Alana *breathes forcefully out. This turns into a laugh.*

Gerry   There . . .

Alana (*laughing*)   Does this count as rape?

Gerry   I'll take it out if / you like.

Alana   Don'tmoveit.

Gerry   Ok.

Alana *winces, whimpers.*

Alana   You're moving it.

Gerry   I'm not. Believe me.

Alana   Oh I'm moving.

Beat.

It's ok.

Beat.

(*Lip quivering.*) Take it out please.

Gerry *does so.* **Alana** *breaks into tears.*

Alana   I'm sorry. I'm sorry. I feel – you know I just, it's like, I don't know but I'm – I'm you aren't I. I'm sobbing. Outside the cave. Oh god and I've got to do it again, go in again. I've got to go in because I've only seen his feet – his toes! You know? And I've got to go in and climb all the way up and how am I going to do that? How do I do it, how does anyone do it? How did they build it! Fucking – ! I don't know . . . It's not possible.

Gerry   It's possible. I'll help you. You'll climb it, of course you will, you'll scale it to the very top. And when you get there you'll look down through the pitch black and everything will be in light and you'll see how you got there and it will be momentous. And it's a gift, an honour to help you do it. To climb to the top and look down with you.

Alana   Why though?

Gerry   Why wouldn't I?

Alana   What's in it for you?

Gerry (*beat*)   That's not the point.

Alana (*to the audience*)   Weeks like this. I didn't go home, or to work sometimes.

During the following they alter the position of their embrace but never fully separate:

Gerry   How is that?

Alana (*to* **Gerry**)   Fine. Slower? Yeah. Ooh it's like it's creaking.

Beat.

I'm sorry I've just realized I'm gripping your balls but I don't think I'm going to let go because it makes me feel more in control of the situation I hope you don't mind.

Gerry   You can, grip my balls. It's only fair.

Alana (*to the audience*)   I didn't change my clothes, I didn't shower.

Alana and **Gerry** *hum together, eyes closed. Eventually* **Alana** *breaks into a fit of giggles.*

Gerry (*eyes still closed*)   This is a sacred meditation it is not funny.

Alana   Yes it is.

Gerry   It's helping isn't it.

Alana (*closing her eyes*)   Yes.

(*To the audience.*)   Sometimes we shared a bath – he had a massive one with feet and everything and the taps on the side so it didn't press into our backs.

Alana *breathes like she's giving birth.*

Gerry   I'm just there, I'm not in.

Alana   Tell me before / you . . .

Gerry   I'll tell you / before I . . .

Alana   Ask me.

Gerry   I'll ask / you.

Alana   Don't go in without / . . .

Gerry   I won't. Trust me.

Alana *nods.* **Gerry** *nods.* **Alana** *nods.*

Gerry   Ok . . .

Gerry *pushes gently.* **Alana** *cries out and moves herself away.*

Alana   Oh I'm sorry.

Gerry   It's alright.

Alana   I'm such an idiot!

Gerry   You're not an idiot.

Alana   You should just give up, it's not fair on you, if I just give up at the littlest – we've done fingers, that's fine, that's all I need. I'm not going to be able – I'll never be able to / manage . . .

Gerry   Alana! I'm still here.

Alana (*to the audience*)   Sometimes he had to leave but we were together every night and every night we would try. Everything.

Gerry (*singing*)   The grand old Duke of York . . .

Alana (*to* **Gerry**)   He had ten thousand men.

Gerry (*singing*)   He marched them up to the . . .

Alana   Gerry . . .

Gerry (*singing*)   He marched them up to the . . .

Alana   Gerry . . .

Gerry (*speaking*)   He marched them up to the.

Alana (*breathes deeply, moans painfully*)   Top of the hill.

Gerry (*singing*)   And he / marched them down again.

Alana (*singing*)   Marched them down again

Gerry   Very good.

(*Singing.*) And when they were / up they were up

Alana (*singing*)   Up they were up

Gerry (*singing*)   And when they were / down they were down

Alana (*singing*)   Down they were down

Gerry and **Alana** (*singing*)   And when they were only –

Alana (*to the audience*)   Incense. Candles. Fucking baby oil, what a mess. Poppers – they made me laugh until I threw up. Nothing worked.

Alana *is convulsing in* **Gerry**'*s arms. He holds her calmly, hiding his worry from her. Eventually she stops.*

Alana (*to* **Gerry**)   . . . See.

Gerry   . . . Wowza.

Psychiatrist   A syncopal attack. It's not a seizure.

Alana (*to the audience*)   Well that's a relief.

Psychiatrist   Not enough oxygen to the brain, most likely from your shallow breathing. You're panicking.

Alana (*beat to* **Gerry**, *laughing*)   'Wowza?'

Gerry   What?

Alana (*laughing*)   Who says Wowza?

Gerry   I do! And it was!

Alana *laughs loudly.*

Gerry   Alana.

Alana   Gerry.

Gerry   Where am I.

After a beat **Alana** *gasps and looks at him, surprised and happy.*

Alana   Oh my god. Wowza!

They laugh.

Alana (*to the audience*)   Nothing except . . . talking. Like I'd never done before, with anyone. And that, just that, felt really good.

Gerry   That's it.

Alana (*to* **Gerry**)   That's it.

Gerry   That's it.

Alana   That's it. Oh god.

Gerry   You're doing it.

Alana   I'm doing it.

Gerry   It's good.

Alana   It's, ok.

Gerry   Do you like it.

Alana   No.

Gerry   I can stop if / you [want me to.]

Alana   Don't stop. Don't – just, finish.

Gerry   You want me to?

Alana   It would help. I think. Positive reinforcement.

Gerry   I love you.

Alana   You don't have to say that.

Gerry   No I don't.

Gerry *comes quietly.*

Alana (*to the audience*)   It went halfway in and halfway out and it took thirty seconds and I hated every moment of it but I did it. I did it. At twenty-five years old, a quarter fucking century, I finally lost my virginity.

Alana *exhales.*

Gerry   How's the view?

Alana (*to* **Gerry**)   Just like you said.

(*To the audience.*) I owe more to him than anyone.

Psychiatrist   And now?

Alana (*to* **Psychiatrist**)   Um. Now . . .

Alana *positions herself on the bed as* **Psychiatrist** *sits facing her, holding a clipboard with few sheets of paper and a pen.*

Alana   Sometimes in the bath now, if I slide forward, well, I don't really feel it then but when I sit back up again I really do – the water, rushing out of me. That's new. Very . . . new, very strange. And nice. And I don't like it. And I smell myself now. More like rain, I smell different. And sometimes not all the wee feels like it's out, feels gone, you know? I don't know what that is, is that just me? Maybe I'm imagining it, anyway, um, little things like that. Change, like that. Make me think – they make me wonder . . . Gerry thinks I was subconsciously denying access to my inner spiritual and emotional worlds to any undeserving lovers, but then he would say that.

Psychiatrist   And you're in a relationship?

Alana   Well we still see each other. We see other people too though. I don't always have sex with them, you know, full sex. Sometimes I can and sometimes I can't. In fact, most of the time I can't. I still can't. Which feels, insane, irritating when I did all that . . . Weird.

Psychiatrist   Weird?

Alana   Yeah. It should be fine now, right. But it's just, not. So I thought, we could, you could help me with that?

Psychiatrist   So you'd say your sex life was active?

Alana   Oh yeah. Yes.

Psychiatrist   And this, issue, doesn't get in the way?

Alana   Yeah so when I'm with someone new I just say: 'Look, I like you, and I think we're getting on well, and it wouldn't be fair of me if I didn't tell you –' and then I tell them.

Psychiatrist   Is that difficult.

Alana   Um, no, it's easy, surprisingly easy to tell them. And then I say 'Feel free to run for the hills' but most don't. Most are ok with it. Most are thrilled I'm up for anal, so.

Psychiatrist   And you enjoy what you do with them?

Alana   Yeah. Yeah I, I come a lot more! Yeah I do. I just know, I know, you know, there's something missing.

Psychiatrist   For you?

Alana   For them.

Psychiatrist   They've told you this?

Alana   No, but . . . I mean, come on.

Psychiatrist *just nods encouragement for her to elaborate.*

Alana   I mean they're guys.

Psychiatrist   Do you consider your womanhood, defined, in a similar way to their manhood? Defined by penetration?

Alana   I don't know what you're getting at.

Psychiatrist   What I'm trying to ascertain is – well, if I can be honest. Why you're here.

Alana   I have vaginismus.

Psychiatrist   Yes.

Alana   And it's a condition, I looked it up, it can be fixed, by people like you.

Psychiatrist   Do you need to be fixed?

Alana   I have vaginismus!

Psychiatrist   Who told you you need to be fixed?

Alana   The internet!

Psychiatrist   Do you want to be fixed?

Alana *can't answer immediately.*

Psychiatrist   Do you feel the need to be fixed?

Alana (*frantic, confused*)   I don't fucking know!

Beat.

Sorry. I didn't – I thought – I thought this would be easier, be the end of it because I'd, you know, done it finally and, and I just told you everything I could think to, to tell you, and I thought you'd tell me now . . . what to do?

Psychiatrist *nods.*

Psychiatrist   The form you filled in, is helpful, thank you. But I'd like you to do a few questions again, with me, this time imagining that men cannot penetrate you. They're physically unable, you live in a world where no one is penetrated, ever, and no one cares. Is that alright?

Alana *nods.*

Psychiatrist   Alright.

(*Reading from a form.*) On a scale from one to five, with five being the most satisfied and one being the least satisfied, how satisfied are you currently with your sexual experiences, generally.

Alana   Uh, without penetration in my vagina, right?

Psychiatrist   Yes.

Alana   . . . Five. Sometimes four, mostly, yeah I guess without that, five.

Psychiatrist   On the same scale where would you place your sexual relationships?

Alana   Four five.

Psychiatrist   And your frequency of sexual encounters?

Alana   Five.

Psychiatrist   Your experience of pleasure during sexual activity?

Alana   Five.

Psychiatrist   I am very happy, Alana, to help you with any issues you are experiencing, any areas of concern, but if your sex life is satisfactory by your own set of measures, not anyone else's, then for us to put you through a program with the intention of normalizing your sexual activity, well I would see that as akin to SOCE.

Beat when **Alana** *doesn't respond.*

Sexual Orientation Change Efforts, Gay Conversion Therapy. There is a danger here, which I'm keen to avoid, of pathologising your sex life. And before going further I would invite you to consider the possibility that your sexual activity may be different or unusual, but still valid.

Alana (*to* **Gerry**)   Everything has changed.

Gerry   Oh dear.

Alana   In a good way.

Gerry   Oh good.

Alana   I had to tell someone and I didn't know who else – it's like I have this new muscle and if I don't keep using it it'll disappear, it's like it's addicting – so I had my session.

Gerry   Oh yes?

Alana   And it was fantastic. I just started talking, and didn't stop, and that felt sort of like a miracle because I'd never told anyone that stuff before but it felt really good to, you know? And they asked me these questions and said these things that made me realise I'd been thinking about the whole thing the whole fucking thing wrong, just totally wrong because I was actually really happy. Actually. I just didn't realise it. Because everyone was telling me what I was missing out on and I felt really shitty about it but those people are just like those Jehova's Witnesses you get at your door, who are really happy with this thing they've got but that doesn't mean you need it too and you believe in god and you're going to start going to church and everything! And it's not their fault, they mean well, they really think they're saving your soul or whatever and that's like me because I was in this constant state of panic and I was like I can't do it, What should I do, What am I going to do, but I realised, it's not that I can't. If I really wanted to, I could. I just, don't, want to. Enough. Anymore. It's just – not worth it. I can get off no problem without doing it, I do all the time now, so why should I go through all that shit every time if I don't want it. Just because everyone else is? Isn't that bullshit? And not everyone else is! There's this woman in America who decided she wasn't going to let herself be penetrated for political reasons and she's fine! And there's this other woman who had to create like her own vaginal passage because she was born without one! And she's fine! And there's all these gay guys who fuck each other in the ass and they're all fine and I'm thinking you know if I was a lesbian no one would give two shits about what I put up myself would they. And then my mind was totally blown I was just standing on the street,

I stopped walking when the thought hit me that it's Just Not A Big Deal. And it's crazy because it was such a big deal for such a long time, everyone makes it such a big deal, and now it's just, not a big deal. For me. Now. After that session. And I wish someone had told me that before all this and I think you know this could actually help other people, I might write a book or a blog or something about it because suddenly, now, I don't feel wrong anymore. Or that I'm missing out on some essential, something. I don't feel like there's this big mystery, or that I've got this awful secret – it's like I've got a different sort of secret entirely, like I've discovered a secret, not that I have one. Do you know what I mean? Am I making sense? It's like, for me, I mean, I don't . . . I don't know what I'm trying to say. What I'm trying to say is, what I want to say is, I have no idea what to do now. Because it's not all mapped out. I thought it was, but it's not. And that's fucking brilliant. Isn't it.

Gerry   Fucking brilliant.

Alana   Fucking brilliant. Fucking. Brilliant.

albatross

for Jodie

Note on the Play

The story of one protagonist was never going to be enough to hold all the ideas I wanted to be in this play. And every time I tried I found the audience were given an out I didn't want them to have: the ability to distance themselves from an individual's decisions or situation ('that would never happen to me / I would never react like that / that's not the world I live in'). So instead I got excited about a story that was communally told, with a web of characters driving it.* Everyone gets a chance to be the protagonist, just as we're all the protagonists of our own lives. Everyone is subject to the chaos of the universe: the actions of others, the consequences of our own actions, and dumb luck. And everyone is closer to the edge than we think; while writing this play I read that 40 per cent of Americans are one paycheck away from homelessness. Writing this now, three years later, that figure is now at 59 per cent. Any stranger could be us, either through the circumstances we're born into or those we make for ourselves. The world as we know it, who we are within it, things we experience as fundamental, could so easily have been so different. So this play is fundamentally about privilege, but that word is only used in the script right at the end, when talking of the privilege of giving a gift. From one stranger to another. From one protagonist to another.

---

* Like one of those party cycle buses – they may take turns at the wheel, but all the characters are pedalling together.

Thanks

This play was made possible and better by Anna Himali Howard, whose intelligence and humanity is in every part of it. I'll be forever grateful to her for her care and kindness, and for getting me the gig in the first place. Thanks also to George Perrin and James Grieve, and to the absolutely stellar original cast: Alpha Kargbo, Charlie Tripp, Lauren O'Leary, Alba Bellugi, Luciana Trapman, Olivia Morris, Olivia Marcus, Sian Maxwell, and Thomas Davison.

Daniel Goldman's production of this play was one of the best things of a terrible year, and it saved my mind. Thanks also to that fantastic cast: Aoife Boyle, Alexandra Kambanella, Joseph Scatley, Joshua Robinson, Rita Estevanovich, Elizabeth Glass, Emily Dermont, Douglas Seldin, and Tom Thornton.

And it has been such a special experience bringing this play to life again with the represent. team. Thank you so much to the incredible cast (Sarel Madziya, Emily Pemberton, Nemide May, Loussin-Torah Pilikian, Samarge Hamilton, Aaron Douglas), Guy Woolf for bringing me on board, and to Jessica Edwards for giving me this gift.

Thanks as always to my crews: Crowther (AW, JB, SH), Playdate (SK, DR, CA, SL, VP), Defectors (KR, RA, AG, TW), and Plant Bangers (RZ, JC, LR, AV, KB, EW). And as always to Jonathan Kinnersley, the best professional decision I've ever made.

Thanks to my family and Geoffrey, who I'm so lucky to have in my life. To Hollie, for her generosity, honesty, and love. And to all the inspirations behind these characters, who I'm privileged to know.

To be an astronaut I apply. To be an astronaut I write a essay.
Everything's done by my choice. But to be born in my country, to
be born in my family, as a daughter of my mom, I didn't do
anything. I was so blessed I were born in the south side – oh thank
god, what if I were born in north Korea. What if I were born in the
middle of the Afghanistan. That is the incredibly lucky part of mine.
All the things that comes from the origin, the moment I were born,
that is total unfair situation, to compare with some kid who were
born in the middle of the war field. Am I the person who deserves
that huge blessing? Or not? Maybe our life is the journey to be the
person who deserves to have that huge blessing when we were born.

Soyeon Yi

no matter what you've done you deserve respect
even if you make mistakes you loveable
doesn't matter your looks, skills, or age, or size, or anything
you're worthwhile
no one can ever take that away from you

Caleb Lawrence 'Kai' McGillvary

The first professional production of *albatross* premiered at The Playground Theatre in London on 20 October 2021, produced by represent. The cast was as follows:

Jodie / Axel	Sarel Madziya
Kit	Emily Pemberton
Jesse / Lucy	Nemide May
Warren / Sunny	Loussin-Torah Pilikian
Pip	Samarge Hamilton
Ashleigh	Aaron Douglas

Creative Team

Director	Jessica Edwards
Assistant Director	Alice Chambers
Set & Costume Designer	Catherine Morgan
Lighting Designer	Bethany Gupwell
Sound Designer	Beth Duke
Assistant Sound Designer	Rose Farbrother
Production Manager	Jack Boissieux
Stage Manager	Joanna Nead & Hannah Hawkins

albatross was first performed at the Royal Welsh College of Music & Drama in Cardiff, on 20 March 2018, as a Richard Burton Company / Paines Plough production. It transferred to London's Gate Theatre on 3 April 2018. The cast was as follows:

Warren	Alpha Kargbo
Jesse	Charlie Tripp
Pip	Lauren O'Leary
Jodie	Alba Bellugi
Axel	Luciana Trapman
Ashleigh	Olivia Morris
Sunny	Olivia Marcus
Lucy	Sian Maxwell
Kit	Arron Cyan

Creative Team
Director	Anna Himali Howard
DSM	Clelia Crawford
ASM	Charlotte Dukes
Designer	Rosalind Mather
Costume Designer	Clara Lockyer
Lighting Designer	Lewis Smith
Sound Designer	Joe Orrell

albatross had a subsequent run at the Rose Theatre. The cast was as follows:

Jodie	Emily Dermony
Axel	Douglas Seldin
Kit	Alexandra Kambanella
Jesse	Tom Thornton
Lucy	Rita Estevanovich
Warren	Joshua Robinson
Sunny	Elizabeth Glass
Pip	Joseph Scatley
Ashleigh	Aoife Boyle

Creative Team
Director	Daniel Goldman
Stage Manager	Natasha Houghton
Technical Manager	Chris Hepburn

Characters

Pip
Sunny *(f)*
Jodie *(f)*
Lucy *(f)*
Axel
Kit
Jesse
Ashleigh
Warren

Key

If a character's line ends with— and their next lines begins with — then the lines run on as one without pause
/ marks a point of interruption
Interrupted lines are still spoken in their entirety
[ ] indicates speech which is not said out loud but is included to clarify the intention of the line
Underlined speech indicates emphasis

The script has been written as flexibly as possible in terms of casting. Characters with (f) should be played by womxn. If pronouns etc in the script are different to those of the actor they can be changed.

KIT
JODIE

jodie   **kit**

I want dice on my neck and
wrapped around the dice,
but not tightly but like like
they're hovering in the grip,
the loose grip, like they're
just about to be tossed, in the
grip of the tail of a snake
which is all green and purple
and red and all these
different colours like a
rainbow but like an oil slick
like at the same time, like
bright but also sort of dark?
and then the snake goes right
the way down my ribs, and i
know that's going to hurt but
i don't care and then on the
other side – it goes around
my belly button like in a loop
de loop like a roller-coaster
and shoots out the other side
where there's its head in the
little curve of my back, and
its jaws are open and out of
its jaws is coming water like
in those japanese paintings
like that style, and it's coming
out like it's fire going all the
way up my back like its neck
is bent upwards so it's
spewing fire onto my back
and out of the fire are spilling
like these little stars and
skulls and roses and they
float down over my arms and
around my collarbone and
they like mist this massive
fuck off albatross on my

chest, with its wings
outspread and its head hung
like this like it's around my
neck and its beak open and
its eyes closed and its feathers
are like beautiful but also sort
of sad and ugly and it's
shining like it's got a halo
behind it like you see in those
christ paintings with the
spikes of light spraying out in
all directions
And that's it basically

Yeah, sounds
It might be, a bit much
For one sitting
But if we could narrow it
down a bit, um, simplify or
Get just one element done
and you can get the rest . . .
Wherever
Great
Cool
So, i like the water idea?

Or the stars and stuff on your
shoulders, i like that
That's some really like classic
imagery
Which is cool

How about we do it this way,
if there was one bit
One element
That was, the most important
to you
If we got rid of everything
else and just kept one, bit
what / would that

The albatross

The albatross?

Great
The albatross, yeah, that's a
badass – can't wear low-cut
tops with that across your
chest though, to work

Ok brilliant
We'll do the albatross
I'll look at some images, i'll
do my – axel's always saying
do your homework so i'll find
some, i'll look up some
depictions, and i'll sketch it
up tonight
Come in tomorrow, early,
we'll do it

JODIE
JESSE

jesse	**jodie**
I'm really sorry i don't have anything	
I've only got my card	
But um	
(*presenting a sandwich*)	
I do have	
I'm not going to eat it	
So if you'd like it	
	(*nods*)
Great	
There	
Great	
Ok	
And i've got some water – i've already swigged from it no you don't want that sorry Let me i could buy you a drink? like a – just there, like a and a like sweet something like a dessert? or something?	

Something?

Um
Could i . . .
Would it be . . .

(*holds out the sandwich*)
A different?
I'm just
Vegetarian
When i can

JESSE
WARREN

jesse
No i don't get it actually, no
i'm sorry, maybe i think i'm
just being, i might just be,
like i can't
Taking in the information
that you're telling me
because i'm panicking
because i – i've paid!

But i like the flights are
booked, i had to give my
passport details!

But i but every but why
would you but there can't be
a problem, you've already
booked it!

Well what i don't really
understand what the
problem is i don't understand

warren

Yes we'll reimburse you

Yes but now we will be
seeking a refund from the
airline, it's unlikely / but
there's no harm in . . .

Yes we did book you on
the excursion not
anticipating there would
be a problem

what it would have have
brought up?

                Well it did it brought up
                that you do have a
                criminal record

I don't though

                You don't have a criminal
                record?

No i don't

                So the dbs did show that
                you do have a criminal
                record

I don't i mean i that's just not
true though

                Well that's . . .
                I don't know what to say to
                that because that's not
                what this shows
                If you want to, i suppose
                you can contest it or . . .

Yeah but not in time right?

                No not in time for this trip
                But you could for another
                trip

But i took i took sabbatical
from work

                I'm very sorry about that

And i had to really negotiate
that because they did not
want to give it to me, i've not
been there – and i said i just
need this specific amount of
time off just to do this specific
thing – *this* thing! this thing
with you! /
And now you're saying

                I understand but we
                cannot have you on the
                trip because of your
                criminal record

I understand but i've / just
told you i've told you though

                I'm sorry yes because they
                have told us – sorry – they

have told us that you have
a criminal record and i'm
afraid we have to act on
that information, over the
information that you're,
giving me

But i'm giving you the truth

Not according to the dbs

But i, i haven't, i don't, i
really don't know what it
It shouldn't
It's been it should be

You want to – a glass of /
water or something
Have a seat

There's been a mistake ok
there's, so, because
There's been a mistake
A mistake
Ok?
A mistake
So, now you, can we just
So there's been a mistake so i
can still come because there's
been a mistake

So i'm / afraid . . .

Theft!
It was theft
Very small theft

Ok
Right, so that is, so you do
have a criminal record?

Yeah

Right

So that's not, that's not, but
that's not, like i didn't,
Kill anybody
You see?

I see but / no i . . .

I didn't i i'm saying
I don't that's not
You care about that?
You don't care about that?

We have to care i'm afraid
We work with very
vulnerable people . . .

Yes but i didn't i didn't uh uh
fuck up any
Vulnerable people!

No but you do have a
criminal record and / for
that reason . . .

Yeah but the criminal –!
Listen, listen, ok, let me –
have you looked?

Have i – me personally?
No
I haven't

Let me tell you exactly what
that was ok, exactly what that
was
I was *fourteen*
That's how long it's been
Like i was barely a teenager
I was technically a teenager
And and i went shopping
Right
I went shopping
With my friends
And i was basically tagging
along like they were basically
doing me a favour
And they stole something
They stole something, from a
vintage shop
They stole this top
Like this shitty top
And they stole it
And they were quite pleased
with it
And then i didn't
immediately say oh yeah
that's cool
So they thought i had a
problem with it and they

were *offended*
So then we went to big multi
whatever and it was massive
and it was really busy and i
just thought you know no
one's going to notice if i take
something from the food bit,
just the food bit
We were getting some like
shitty sweets like really posh
sweets but they were like so
posh that they didn't taste
good and
And i just thought i'll just
take some
And that will show
And also this place is like
Massive
They're not going to care
About like a bar of chocolate
going
And so i put this bar of
chocolate
Down my top
Thinking it wouldn't be seen
there
And then i got all the way out
of the food bit, all the way out
the front doors, and *that's*
where someone stopped me
Like they waited til i got –
like it was it was right at the
– i was so certain that i was
going to make it before they
said excuse me and they like
brought me aside and those
– my friends
My friends just
Laughed
At me
And they didn't wait for me
And they went the whole way,

on a fourteen year old, they
went the whole way
And i had to go to these
classes
And it was just an awful part
of my life and i was so angry
for such a long period of time
because
I had thought it was a
victimless crime
You know what i still think it
was a victimless crime
I didn't hurt anyone
I just did this shitty stupid
one-off thing, once
And i've had jobs and no one
has bothered
No one has cared about this
Before you
'Cause i'm not a violent
I just want to be
And now you're saying
I mean come on you can't be
saying

                                I'm afraid that's what i'm
                                saying

I – !
I've – !
I've been posting about this!
I got all those donations!

                                Well listen, i do
                                understand, i
                                I i i'm quite full on, right
                                now
                                Sorting everything out
                                For the trip
                                But
                                So it . . .
                                If this, this is the end of
                                our conversation about the
                                matter, for this trip
                                And

I think we should say
goodbye
At this point /
We can . . .

I don't think we should say
goodbye
I think
I think you should give me
another chance
I think you should
I think
'Cause this is what the whole
thing is about right?
It's about bettering yourself
And showing
And proving
And
Finding
The best part of yourself
And
Expanding that part and
being nice and giving
something
To other people
I think you should let me do
that i think you should let me
help 'cause you're going to be
one man down right?
You can't, 'cause – this is such
short notice
Why is this such short notice!
Why didn't you tell me
earlier!

We didn't tell you because
we didn't know ourselves,
we always book
Book the places, before
the dbs – which takes a
very long time to go
through – goes through
completely
Uh and because frankly
we've never had this

before, we've never had
someone apply to be part
of the programme and
then
Lie about their status

I didn't lie abut anything, i
didn't, i
Really did not / think that this
would

Well you were wrong
These are very at-risk
people that we're going to
work with
And this might be
For you
About bettering yourself
But for me, for this
institution it's about
bettering themselves, their
situation, it's about
helping them better
themselves, to be more
accurate
It's not about you
It's not about your second
chance
I have to, consider, the
wellbeing of the people we
are there to help
Not the wellbeing of
someone who can afford to
take time off work to go do
this
To to
Be a better person
And honestly
I i we have more cause for
upset than you because
you are correct
Because that is true, it is
very late
And we are now a man
down

And we will just have to
make do with that because
you
Were dishonest

I was not
Dishonest
Or
I had no idea i was being
Dishonest
Ok?
I thought
I had no idea i was being
dishonest
It shouldn't be there
It shouldn't be there at all!

I don't think we can
resolve this in a, in this
conversation, to a degree
that you will be happy with
Or me
So i would like to say
goodbye, now
And i
You can email ashleigh, let
me write down their – let
me email them right now
in fact and say what's
happened
And you can continue this
conversation with them,
i'll cc you in

No listen
Listen
I get it
The rules are there for a
reason i'm sure some
Dipshit has been a dipshit
before with you

No we have not had
anything like this

Well you're not going to get it
with me

I'm not going to be a dipshit,
ok?
I'm going to be a good
person, that's the whole
reason for this
It is, for me
To get to be a good person
You can just
I get that you have to
But this doesn't have to
You can
You can just make the
reasonable decision now
Ok?
You can just go with your gut
Just go with your gut and
trust that i'm who i say i am
That i'm a good person
That that
That that
That that thing
In the shop
Is not who i am
That that was a blip
On an otherwise like a
straight line
That i
Won't fuck you over
I promise i won't

Look i
If it was up to me
Honestly
But
Look
I hear what you're saying
But
Ok
But
So
So i am not in a position
I don't know you
You seem

Like a genuine person
You seem nice
But i
I want to
But
And this is a neutral
statement
I have no reason to believe
you

WARREN
PIP

warren   **pip**
I don't know when they got
married
I don't
So i think it was
Three years
Before they had me
That they got married
But i'm not, sure
But they were really young
Really really young
And
And in fact they met
At university
And my mum
She, has just moved there
because she's not from there
Uh my dad who is from there
And my mum she joins a a
A gym
And my dad is at that gym
As she's going she's getting
like the
Welcome tour or something
And my dad is at the
reception where she gives
her her
Well she says hello or
something or she's just

finished signing in or
something
And
They like
Nod at each other i think
Maybe they chat i'm not sure
Um
He
Turns to the person behind
the counter – who he knows,
that's right, so she's his friend
At the reception he knows
the person working on
reception
Uh and says if you
Give me
That woman's number
And we get married
I'll give you my, jacket
But it was like a special jacket
like it was some sports jacket
not a sports jacket like the
fashion but like he was part
of some sports club
And
Uh this is it's a big deal for
some reason
Uh but anyway she says yes
and this is, she's not meant to
do this
Maybe it's illegal
It doesn't matter she's not
meant to do it and she does
And
My dad calls, my mum
And asks her on a date
And
The point is
Ten days later they're
engaged
And
They're still together

Today now
They're still together
Um
Because i asked my parents
once
Separately, i asked them
Why did – *why*
Why did you
Get engaged
After ten days!
Like who says yes to that why
was that
Why did that – why did you
say yes
Um
And my mum said <u>i kissed a</u>
<u>lot of frogs</u>
Which is like very her
And my dad
Said
<u>You know</u>
<u>On day nine</u> or something
<u>I did some basic mathematics</u>
<u>And figured that from what i</u>
<u>knew of your mother</u>
<u>That she was 75% perfect</u>
Like it wasn't a romantic
number
Maybe it was 80
It doesn't matter
Let's say 80% perfect
<u>Your mum was 80% perfect</u>
<u>and the 20% that wasn't</u>
<u>Was</u>
<u>Stuff i could deal with</u>
<u>Stuff i could work at</u>
<u>That</u>
<u>20% was located in an area</u>
<u>that was not a deal breaker</u>
<u>for me</u>
<u>And</u>
<u>Relationships</u>

<u>Successful relationships</u>
<u>Are choosing, to work</u>
<u>At least 20%</u>
<u>So i thought i should you</u>
<u>know i could wait</u>
<u>To find someone 5% better</u>
<u>than your mum or i could say</u>
<u>you know what i'm going to</u>
<u>choose</u>
<u>To love this person</u>
And i
Want to choose to love you
I want to choose
You
And i think – i've given it a
lot of thought and i think
I *think*
And maybe i'm wrong maybe
it'll turn out that i'm wrong
But i do i really do think
That that
I mean
It feels like 50% but let's say
– let's keep with the 20%
That 20% of you
That did that
This whole
Situation
Is 20% that i think i can deal
with
I think it's not a deal breaker
I think i can work for this
20%
If you can
And i want to try and i am
Saying
I know it's probably
surprising but
Just some things have got me
thinking and
Like at work and
This thing

Just recently
And
I'm saying i want to try
And i
And
If you want to try
Too
We can start again

No
No

PIP
AXEL

axel
I have had a day

pip

Oh yeah?

Oh yeah
Yes

Well, tell me about it

Well first kit didn't show up
Prick
Had a customer today
A fucking booking
And just didn't show up
And i was
Mortified
'Cause i'd set it up
And i look like the prick

That's shit

And i had four name requests

Fuck that

Exactly
And i had one very dark lady
who wanted a very small and
very detailed and i tried to
tell her but she wouldn't
listen but it's going to look
like shit in not long, you
know

I know

And then i had someone
Who wanted their girlfriend
on their arm
And i was like no
names unless they're
dead dude And he was
like oh she is
But i could tell he was just
saying that
And i went are you sure
about this dude
And he was like of course
i'm sure i wouldn't do it if
i wasn't sure
So that felt weird, but i did it
I'm not about to put up a sign
Let them make their own
mistakes
So it's just been a lot of things
today
How was your day?

Oh it was
Fine
I mean
It wasn't great

At work?

Yeah
I had to do something i
hated
Something i
Just an unfortunate . . .
Anyway glad it was me at
least and not someone
who didn't know them
having to
And, i, well, i'm staying
with ashleigh, and
everything's fine there,
they just you know they
asked again when i was

moving
Which is fair
So i just started looking
today and thinking you
know where can i
afford and *there's not
many places*
Um and uh
Well there are a few but it's
like a really big step
From what i'm used
to And i know that's um
my own fault
So um
Yeah i'll just have to i'll just
have to take one
So that was a bit of a
bummer to be honest, just
looking through all the
listings and thinking
*Well fuck it it'll have to be one
of you then won't it*

Yeah that sucks
Well look i'll keep my ear to
the ground for you
Do you
Want me to post about it on
facebook like see if anyone's
looking?

Uh
Yes! yes that would be
great
Yeah
Um actually i was um
I mean stop me if this is
But uh
Yeah i was just thinking
Because you've got um
Quite a lot of living space
and i don't have much,

stuff
Um
I was thinking
I was well i was wondering
if that was something
you're interested in

Oh, i would be
But actually, i've got my
brother
Actually my brother
sometimes sleeps on that
couch so it has to be
free, for him, because
You know every so often he
just needs to not be alone
And i need to be able to, i
would hate to not be able to
provide that for him

I wasn't actually um,
talking about the couch
I was, i was not thinking of
the couch

Yeah i know you weren't
I don't know why i pretended
i didn't
Sorry, that's not truthful
That's disingenuous

I
Don't
Think
That i would like that

Ok, no, that's,
absolutely fine, and um
i you know i only – i
haven't asked before
this point because i
thought, i just didn't
want to put any
pressure or anything

and um i figured that
you would offer and
you didn't and that's
why i didn't ask but
now it's just you know
i'm looking at *all* the
options now, um, and
trying to figure out
which is best so that's
that's that's why uh i
am sorry i put this in
front of you, i didn't
mean to, make this
awkward
Um
Is it 'cause is it is it is it
because your brother
doesn't, know?

He, doesn't know, but that's,
that's not why

Ok
Wh-why?

Why?

Yeah why?

Well
Because i think that's a step
For us
That's really serious
And i
Don't know if it's a step
That
I want to happen

You don't know if you
want it to happen?

No

What ever?

Well
Right now

But eventually?

I don't know

Ok
That's fair
Just just so we're being,
just while we're being clear
Um
I do
I really do
Not least of all because i
want this to be, successful
*Because if it's successful, in a
way, it's all ok!*
But uh i do
So now you have that
information now

Great thank you
That's good to have that
information

Ok
And i would hope that
Um you know, i'm in a
bind
And i was really hoping
you could help
Seeing as
Um
I'm not saying
I'm not placing blame
I'm just saying you're in a
position to help
I mean i spent a lot of time
over there anyway

You did yeah

Yeah i did

So
When do you think you
will know?

So while we're being honest

Please

Yeah while we're being
honest

I
Think actually i do know
That that is not a step i will
want to take with you

Right
Wow
Ok
Uh
Sorry
That is fine for you to say
I'm just i was just – it's not
a wow like
Fuck you wow
Although
Um
Well fuck ok
I feel fucking stupid
I don't know why i feel
stupid
Why should i feel stupid
because i
I thought that's what, you
know, you never gave any
indication that's not where
this was going

Well no there was no reason
to give any indication that's
not where it was going

Right so when did it stop
going, that way

Well i just
Thought about it
I've given it a lot of thought
I try to give everything a lot
of thought, you know i do
And i have come to a point of
clarity about our relationship
and i don't think it's
sustainable
And that is not your fault, it's
not my fault, it's just the way
it is

So i would rather not
Go down a path that leads to
sustainability when that
sustainability would actually
be a trap

A trap!

I'm sorry that was
I mean
I can't think of a better word
But that's not what i mean
but
That's as accurate as i can,
get

This is insane
Why – when did you
When, did this moment of
clarity arrive?

A little while ago
We haven't seen each other
much

Well i've been kind of busy
dealing with the fallout!

I'm sorry that you have had
to deal with that

Have you not had to deal
with it?

To be honest no
Not much
We don't have a lot of mutual
friends

We have some mutual
friends

Yeah but they're all
peripheral friends
So they're not, core friends

What do my friends
think?

What do your friends think?

Yeah because i have lost
friends

I am so sad about that
My friends

I don't know what they think

What you haven't told
them?

I've told some
And
They have been
Empathetic

Fuck me well can you, take
a leaf out of their book or
something?

Look, i
Understand why this is
hurtful to you

No i don't think you do
I don't think you
understand the extent
because this has had
serious ramifications on
my life and
It seems to have not
touched you in the
slightest not even put
ripples on your surface so
I
Want help from you
Because we are not even in
this and we should be

Well i don't agree with that

Sorry?

I don't agree we should be
even in this

How are we not even in
this!
You and me did this
equally

Well the thing is
I don't think that's true

How do you not think
it's–!
Please explain yourself
I i am, i feel like
I am dreaming or tripping

or both, right now
Like this is a come down
nightmare

Fuck off with that

You do look tired

No you do i don't think this is
a good time maybe we should
/ another time maybe . . .

This is a fine time i want
this, this is the time, i'm
fine to do this now

Are you really sure /
because i just feel . . .

No i'm sure i'm sure i want
to know why you think
even though we did
exactly the / same thing
that somehow we're not
equals somehow

Not exactly the same thing
We're not equal
Because i had not made the
Same commitment as you
Because i was not in a
relationship
And you were
You had, this person
That you were betraying
Sorry that's a charged word
but it's the most accurate
thing i can come up with
And i was not betraying that
person

Look
You fucked me, and i
fucked you, so you are also
the bad guy here
I don't see why i'm the
only one getting
punishment
I'm the only one getting
punishment for the thing
we did together

Well i think when i was doing
it

The stakes were not the same
The investment was not the
same
As when you were doing it

But you knew i had a
boyfriend

Yes
But he wasn't my boyfriend

How . . .
Ok
This literally makes no
sense
You are literally making
zero sense

I am not the one
Who has made the decision
To have an affair

But you have made the
decision!
To have – to be part of the
affair!

Right

Yes!
So how are they different!

Because i'm not – because i'm
single

That is –!
But you are, going back a
a a
Community promise
Not to
You – you are a fucker!
And you're behaving like a
fucker! right now!

I don't think i'm behaving
like a fucker
I think you're being really
unfair
I'm getting really upset now

You – how – how is this-!
You've been such a twat
this whole time!

But listen
But listen
You are the cheater
I am not a cheater
And i really like you
I like you a lot
But i also like myself
And i also have to look out
for myself
And the fact is
I can't trust you

When did we meet?

I don't understand the
question

As in do you remember
the month? do you
remember the month?

No

It was hot though

Yes /

And that was, an exciting
thing so it was like, the
first few hot days or
something, of the year
It was like new hot, it was,
early summer i think

Yeah that's right /

And then how long, was it
til we slept together the
first time

Well that was at the gig

Exactly
You waiting
Doesn't / affect

That's not what i'm saying /

Let me, let me finish
Just don't, just do me a
favour and don't say
anything

Well i, you were asking me
questions

Ok but i'm not anymore so
just shut up til i'm stopped
So it was that period of
time
And i, i wanted to fuck you
from the beginning, from
the first day, from early
summer
Ok?
And then we fucked for
Half a year, ish?
Before i said anything
But i did say it
We didn't get found out
There was no, walking in,
or
Found texts
Or anything like that
I said something
Because i loved warren,
actually
And you didn't want me to
You are not a cheat
You are worse
You're a hypocrite

And you get to walk away

AXEL
KIT

kit
I was just sick, i was just sick,
axel

axel

What do you mean you
were just sick? what kind
of sick? i want to know the
details of your sickness, i
want to know how many
times you sicked up and
what came out and what
volume

No i wasn't i just didn't feel
good /

    Didn't feel good? well why
    I mean listen all of that is
    fine, you just need to let
    me know
    Ok?
    You just need, so i can talk
    to – you know that
    homeless woman came?
    you had an appointment
    That homeless woman you
    / had an appointment

Uhuh yeah   With – yeah – she was
Yeah   waiting for you, we were
    both waiting for you, i had
    people waiting for me
    It was a, shitshow, man
    It was a shitshow /

I know   It was a shitshow – no you
    don't know you weren't
    there
    I had to deal with all your
    shitty outcomes, yeah?
    And i
    And listen
    You just need to be better
    at communicating ok?
    Alright? now how are you
    feeling now?

I'm fine today

    Ok so it was a twenty-four-
    hour thing?

Yeah

    Alright 'cause you look
    fine

I am fine, i'm fine now

    Ok
    I'm glad
    So listen this is her
    number, ok
    Call her – she has a phone

thank god make another
appointment
Beggars can't be – maybe
that's insensitive but, i
think it's going to be ok

I i think i'm not going to do
that
I
I was thinking, i was thinking
actually
I was thinking
Maybe i shouldn't
Maybe if you wanted to do
the tattoo maybe that would
be better

Are you pussying out?
Don't pussy out you're
going to be fine, it's / going
to be fine

I'm not pussying out, i'm not
pussying out

Or is [*it*] – look just
because she's sleeping
rough – that's what makes
her / perfect for a free one!

No that's not what this is so I
just i'm not comfortable with
her tattoo

I'm not comfortable with the
Um
The albatross

What?

Yeah

The bird?

I mean
Sure the detail . . .
What aren't you
comfortable with?

You know where that is from?

The – what? like the sky?

No like the albatross
Around your neck

So it's not a phrase, it's a

I know the phrase

book, it's a story, it's a story,
it's the mariner story

                    Ok

Yeah

                    So, what?

So he shoots, the bird
He shoots the bird and then
has to wear it round his neck
for the rest of his well for the
rest of the story

                    Fine?

Yeah so what so
Why does she want an
albatross round her neck?

                    Who gives a shit?

No because you know why
what if, what if she's really
dangerous?
You know, what if she's
Maybe that's why she's
homeless

                    Dangerous look at her she
                    was fucking tiny, i could
                    take her

That's not that's that's not
what i mean i mean what if i
what if i fuck up and then,
she's / she

                    A, you are not going to
                    fuck up
                    B, this is bullshit
                    C, it's just a fucking bird
                    just draw the fucking bird
                    Put it on her
                    It's fine

I don't i'm not, i don't want
to do it
I don't want to be part of it
I don't want to put it on her

                    You're serious about this

No
No
Uh-uh
You're going to have to get
over this
I'm not doing that fucking
tattoo for you, you are
doing that fucking tattoo
You are calling her
You are rearranging

I don't want / to

You have to
You have to get over this
You have to if you
You know you keep you
keep
Pestering me
To let you
If you want to level up if
you think you're ready
you've got to
Who do you think our
fucking clientele is
Huh?
This. is who. we work for
Everyone's got a
Alright everyone's done
things
You understand that?
And they shouldn't have to
– it's not fair
If she wants to tattoo this,
on her chest
That's up to her
It's not your job that's her
job
You don't get to decide
what that is for her
Ok?
You are making that

appointment
And you are giving that
person that tattoo, because
no matter what they've
done
The person looking at you
The person in the moment
Is your client
And don't – and look if
you have a problem with
that, if that's difficult for
you then get out my shop
It's too embarassing for
me
It's too fucking
embarassing

KIT
ASHLEIGH

kit
It's what got me into this, so
In a way i'm sort of glad it
happened

Yeah i mean yeah, i mean
what happens
The universe has a way of, i
think, giving you, and you've
just got to trust it
Everything that happens
makes you who you are
doesn't it

Yeah it is good isn't it
You do get what you paid for
that is true

Not as much as i thought
Um scar tissue is pretty thick
so it just it took a long time i

ashleigh

Oh no
No no

You really can hardly tell

Did it hurt?

had to go back a few times
Um, and the ink, interacts
with scar tissue differently
Anyway that's what i'm sort
of specialising in i guess
Um
Scar, coverage and, stuff like
that
'Cause, you know i got
experience and then i can
talk to people about their
experience and we can be
you know, they can trust me
and we can just share that
So that's good

                              Yeah that's really good

Yeah so it's sort of a
Usp i guess

                              I was actually asking about
                              the burn though

Oh yeah, yeah it hurt   Were you recovering a
                              long time?

It does take a long time yeah
Actually, so
The recovery i remember
That
I mean
Just because it lasted so long
and was so
Awful
Constant
Awful
But i can't remember the
pain of the actual burn now
Um
I can just remember that i
was in pain
I just can't conjure it, you
know?

                              Yeah
                              Lucky really

I guess yeah

Yeah sure

Yeah yeah
(*positions themselves better*)

Mm?

Well the whole place went up

No not the whole – the arm
This place, here
And a bit on my back

Well
It's weird because i mean
there was smoke everywhere
but um, this wasn't,
specifically
You know, you think things
are on fire and they have
flames or like they're red or
something but this, must
have, just
It didn't have any outward –
it must have just, contained,
all the heat
Secretly?
It didn't look like it was on
fire
And i knew i had to be low on
the ground so that's why i got
But then the ground was bur
– was burning me
So, i felt like um
Like i was fucked i was
doomed like i was gonna die
Because i was

Like childbirth

Can i touch it?

(*fingers the tattoo like braille*)
I don't get it

Sorry i still don't
understand, how it
happened?

The whole building?

How did it get to you?

You're told, to get really low
because of the smoke and
And then that was burning
me
Once i'd done that
Ah sorry ah fuck sorry
I don't talk about it as a rule,
it's a bit difficult

                                        Yeah, sorry

No don't you be sorry

                                        No i am sorry / i shouldn't

No i mean *i'm in control*
It's just
You asked, i want to tell you
It's not like
They did such a good job
You have to look so closely
don't you, to know what's
underneath
And fuck, the relief, you
know?
I could be this other person
now, or just a person
Just a person
Not this thing (*the burn*)
But this whole thing (*their whole self*)
But that's the thing about
tattoos they cover you up but
they remind you
Because you put a pretty
flower over it but it's still
someone's self harm scars or
their abusive boyfriend or
stupid sixteen year old
mistake or whatever
It is but it isn't
It's weird
I don't know

                                        I'm so sorry

Don't be silly! no i didn't
mean to, go off like a twat
about it, sorry

I am though

I don't mind talking, i
promise
Has it, has it killed the
The mood

No! no no
Nooo
It's sexy
You're all
Beautiful and broken
And i can
No it's hot
(*grimaces at the word choice*)

(*laughs*)

(*laughs*)

(*kisses ashleigh*)

(*kisses back*)

I like this

I like this too
(*kisses kit*)

(*kisses ashleigh*)

What was more painful,
the tattoo or the recovery?

Oh the recovery definitely
(*kisses asheigh*)
Tattoos are fine
(*kisses ashleigh*)

(*kisses back*)

I've only had henna
For a wedding once
And you know temporary
stick on
And then, sharpies, like in
the sixth form common
room

That's where it starts

Were you always an artist?
Were you really good at /

Oh no i wasn't a fucking artist
I wasn't a fucking anything to
be honest
It's less about that really it's
more about
You just train your muscles,
you just um
Practise, like anything, you
just practise
That's all it is, really

                        art at school?

I promise, i promise
Anyone can do it
You just have to, you know
i'm really lazy
And i care about this just
enough to
Make me make myself get
good at it
I'm good at a lot of things . . .
as it happens . . .

                        I don't believe that

                        Oh yeah?

Yeah yeah
I'm uh . . .
I'm good at . . .
I'm good with my hands

                        (*laughs*)

(*kisses ashleigh*)

                        (*kisses back*)
                        What's your favourite
                        tattoo you've ever done?

Uh . . .
I don't have a favourite
I mean i like tattoos in weird
places
Because you get to see
people's weird places . . .

                        Yeah it must be harder,
                        right?
                        Do you ever, have to like
                        tattoo someone's anus?
                        like the hole?

No i have never tattooed
someone's anus
Do you want to be my first?

Uh . . . no

Are you sure? i'm sure you
have a beautiful anus, we
could do something really
special there i'm sure
(*pawing ashleigh*)

(*laughs*)

Can i just, let me just, look at
the anal region to see . . .

What's the worst tattoo
you've ever – no – have
you ever refused a tattoo?
no – have you ever done a
gang tattoo?

Uh i have not – i'm still an
apprentice
Though i
Anyway
No i haven't

Ok well has, have you ever,
like does your boss have
gang tattoos?

No! no my boss, no my boss is
basically, my boss would be
on wall street if they could be
And this is just what they're
doing
No i haven't, we don't do that
stuff
It's funny you ask actually
I've been asked to
To give this tattoo and
My boss wants me to and i
don't
I think – well normally i'd
think it was just about the
money for them
But
This isn't, this is going to be a
free tattoo because i'm an

apprentice *and also*
The person is homeless
So *they can't pay*
Um yeah
Just a bit
I don't know
I think they're going to force
me
So that's on my
(*about ashleigh*) This is a nice
distraction
From that

Why don't you want to
give it?

Oh just the imagery
Basically

What is it like a pussy on a
pussy or something?

(*laughing*) A what on a what?

I don't know just
something gross or like
Or is it like some donkey
fucking a child or
something?

Oh my god no, no it's not
that

Well what is it! go on tell
me!
I'm just thinking of bad
shit! just tell me!

It's uh . . . a big bird

Big Bird?

No a bird bird, a big bird

A big bird?
Why don't you want to do
that?

Well it's an albatross actually

Is that a gang symbol?

No – you and gang [*symbols*]
– no it's the imagery of the
albatross is um, something
weighing on you, for the rest

of your life, some awful thing
And i just don't feel
comfortable because i don't
know what the awful thing is
And i don't think we should
have that person in our shop
And you know what if i do it
wrong
And they do something, an
awful thing, to me?

Oh
I've got you

And you know i'm really
picky about my clients

You don't have clients

What?

You're an apprentice
right?

Yes
I still have clients

Oh, but you haven't been
paid

No but i've tattooed people
That's the whole part of the
apprenticeship is to tattoo
people /

For free

Right
For free
But they're still my clients

Right

So any[way] – so i'm really
picky about my clients
because you know it's an
expression of them but it's
also an expression of me and
we've got to be really on the
same page and i've got to be
totally comfortable because
you know that's the that's the
best thing about the this job
is that your art – i mean i'm

not an artist but i i am i guess
i am making art and, your,
work, is literally living
somewhere, it's literally living
. . . art
And so that's gonna, be out
there forever like paintings
you can destroy if you don't
like them
Or you change your mind
and you can't . . .
Once it walks out the door it's
you
And
I i don't think i want
Me
To be on this person

She

Yep

Oh yeah

Um it it's different from
culture to cul[*ture*] – but
basically yeah, it is yeah, can
be

He's homeless right?

Right ok
She's homeless?

I heard this radio play
about homelessness once
and it had like this
character who had like
tears tattooed on his face

Yeah
Which is like people
you've killed right?

So, it was about a character
who had that
And then right at the end
it was revealed that they
just got that when they
became homeless
So that people would be

scared of them
And wouldn't fuck with
them and steal their shit

Oh
Smart

Yeah so i'm thinking what
if she's trying to do that?

Make people afraid of her?

Yeah

I . . .
Yeah maybe
But then why does she want
people afraid of her

Because she's a homeless
woman
She's in danger all the
time
Has she been homeless a
long time? like does she
look it?

Look homeless/?

Yeah

I mean
No she just looks
She looks
Like a hitchhiker more

Like someone on their gap
year?

No like, like
You know the guy on
youtube who was like
Smash smash smash – that
guy?

What?

There's a video of a guy in a
you know one of those like
local broadcast interviews
and then they autotune it
Anyway he goes smash
smash smash!
Anyway he was hitchhiking
– she looks like a hitchhiker

Ok
No
I don't know that, um
Well
Is she like, unwell?

She had a pretty crazy idea
for a tattoo

Actually it was a much bigger
tattoo and i got her to narrow
it down, to the albatross

The albatross

Oh so this is
So you'd like
Had a consultation with
her?

Yeah

You'd suggested the
albatross?

No no that was all her

So but you said you would
do it and what now you're
not going to do it?

Well yeah any time a
customer comes in and wants
something that we don't
agree with we have the right
to refuse service

But your boss wants you to
do this, he knows about
the albatross?

Yeah they, they know

Ok
So they don't see a
problem with it

No but again
I don't know i
I just don't want to do it
That's all there is to it
We don't have to talk about it
I'm / ruining the mood again

Have you asked her about
the tattoo?

What do you mean?

Like what it means

No i haven't

Why not?

Because maybe i don't want
to know

But it might be about
nothing

But she could also be lying

Yeah but anyone could be
lying

Yeah but i mean she's more
likely to lie

Why?

Because she's
Now listen
I am fine with homeless
people
Like when those spikes were
put outside my local shop i
signed a petition because
that's that's dreadful
I know it's not their fault
that's not – i know it's not
necessarily their fault
But
At the same time
Sometimes
I just think
You know what if what if
she's been to prison
Like what if actually that's
why she's homeless
I'm not saying
And you know on the train,
actually yesterday i was on
the train and there was
someone
Begging
And they asked me
specifically for one pound
forty

They were like i need one
pound forty i'm one pound
forty away from a hostel for
tonight so i gave them two
pounds a two pound coin
Like more than they needed
And then they went on a bit
to the next person and asked
for one pound forty again!

So homeless people lie is
what you're saying?

I'm just saying they have
more reason to lie
Than someone / else who's
paying

Well it takes balls to get on
a train and ask for money
I know, i've done it

Really?

When i was young
Younger
Mostly as an existential
exercise
But i stopped because i
realised
I could afford to do that
And other people couldn't
afford not to
And that was fucked up
You're not someone who
like says don't fund their
drug habit or whatever?

No no give them money of
course fuck you know they're
adults / they can

I always give them money

Right yeah we should that's
not / what i'm

So isn't the tattoo like that
then?

Ok i
I think i maybe have upset
you

You haven't upset me

No i think i have
And i think maybe we should
just drop it and
I think maybe i should just go

You don't have to go

Yeah, i do, because i think i
think you think i should do
the tattoo
And so does my boss
And fuck it maybe you're
both / right but i

Look just, let's just, just
come back here

No no, i think, i'm, i'm gonna
go

Don't go, don't go
You don't know what i
think

I do, i can see it, on your in
the way you're holding your
lips
You think i have to do the
tattoo don't you
Because i agreed or whatever

I don't think it's whether
you
I think you should
The question is not do you
have to
The question is should you

Right that's what i mean
though / isn't it

The question is can you
live in clean conscience if
you don't

What do you think

What do i think?

Yeah

I think
You'll be happier
And less stressed about it /

Ok i'm not stressed about it

Ok alright
I see what you
But i am not trusting the
universe right now
I am trusting a person
A stranger
And it's not fair, i don't think
it's fair, to say
Because trust
Is something you earn
Not something you give, not
something you risk, ok?

Right

We know each other
We've met up, come on, how
many times now

Yeah but that's a huge
question

I have upset you
I'm going

I don't know

if
If
You trust the universe

So you should only trust
people that you know and
have earned your trust?

Well if that was true i
would never date again
I don't know you
You don't know me

Yeah but can you ever
really know someone?

Yeah but you're you're
asking huge questions!
Aren't you!

How did the fire start?

Really?

Really

Because they do a report
don't they?
They go in and find out
They can always tell
I think that's amazing
I heard this podcast
It's amazing how they can
find out how it happened
And they never told you?

They might have told my
parents but i was too young
at the time
They maybe just didn't tell
me

Ok

'Cause it's funny 'cause i
would have thought . . .
'Cause you've got this
thing you've got to carry
With you forever now
And i thought you said
you fell

The first time
You said
You fell

I didn't start that fire

I'm not saying you did

You're implying it

I
I don't mean to imply

Do you know if it was
accidental, or?
On purpose? The fire?

I don't know anything

Yeah trust is funny isn't it

I think it was accidental
I think
I'm just guessing
I don't know
I think it was just a mistake

Yeah
It's a weird line right
Between a mistake and a
fuck up
Like one
You get away with
And one you don't
One affects others / and
I'm going to go   one just . . .
I'm sorry if you landscaped
or something for this

For what?

For us
For sex

We weren't going to have
sex
Read a room

ASHLEIGH
LUCY

ashleigh   **lucy**
(pleasant)
Hi, sorry, um, we know each
other
I just don't know how

(also pleasant)
Oh, no, i don't think so

We've definitely met, um
Do you know do you know

greg? maybe it was at his
wedding, because i don't feel
like we've talked
I feel like we've been
introduced but not, uh, you
know just for like two seconds
at a bar or something?

I do not know, a, greg
Uh well i do know a greg
but i . . .
Greg walton?

(shakes head no)

Yeah i didn't think you'd
know him
Um
I
Sorry, who are you?

Sorry! i'm ashleigh

Hi ashleigh
I'm lucy

Right
Lucy . . .
Lucy . . .
Uh

Lucy benice

Lucy benice . . .
Do you know julia?

No – well, i mean, julia
who?

Sure julia tsu

Julia tsu
No i don't

Do you know . . .
Did you do the colour run!

The what?

The where you run through
all the colours

Oh the like marathon
thing?

Yes

No

Ok

Saved your clothes then –
they do stain
Um
I mean we have definitely
met
I mean, do you have any
thoughts?

I really don't because i
don't think we know each
other

I am just sure of it
I'm sorry i don't want to be
awkward or anything / but i
just think i'll think of it and
kick myself / like
four hours after this and
you'll be gone by then

No it's not awkward

It's a little awkward
I
So i
I am in porn
Maybe you've seen me in
porn

That is it

Right

Yeah that is awkward i'm so
sorry
I'm so sorry i pushed it i was
just so certain /

It's ok /

Oh my god i'm
remembering, you being
introduced to the camera
That's what that is /

It's really not a big deal
It happens, sometimes
Not all the time

I bet it happens all the time

Not all the time

Ok
Well
It was great to meet you i am
so sorry

Don't, no, don't worry

I
So
But that was a long time ago
now?

Sorry?

I just i
You look really different like
you looked much younger
Is that makeup or?

Uh no no it's been a long
It's been a long time

Right, sorry
You probably have a whole
new identity
Um

Um
Sort of

Sorry you probably don't like
people bringing it up like
you've – like you know it is so
hard because it's all online
and you can't do anything on
the internet without it being
there forever like plastic, i'm
sure this is so embarassing
i'm so sorry i'll shut up

It's not embarassing
Why would it be
embarassing

Uh no reason no that's not
what i meant uh no it
shouldn't be embarrass-you
shouldn't be embarrassed of
course
Um
What did i mean, i just meant
(*struggles*)
Help me out here

I know what you meant
I'm sorry
Um no i am in fact i am

Starting again
I'm doing – i'm starting up
again
I'm, having a comeback

Oh!
Cool!
Is that a pun?

Uh
No

Ok
Great! hey! that's fantastic

Yeah thank you

So you, is that, what is, i don't
know what that's, like at all, i
don't know, i don't even
know what questions to ask
about that

It's ok it's just, i'm just, i
decided to start again

Ok

Yeah so i've got some
shoots lined up with some
people i used to work with
who aren't thankfully out
of the business or dead so
um
So no basically no it's not
embarrassing actually i'm
at a really exciting place in
my life
So that's, yeah

Gotcha
Well, good luck
Not that you need it, i'm sure
you're great
I mean i know you're great

So you have an appointment?

I do yeah, yeah

I am getting i have

I have an std
Um

Right

And they want to stop my
medication but when i stop
my medication i get really
bad flare ups
It's just debilitating i can't
work so that's why i'm here
to make sure they don't stop,
that

Yeah you've really got to
stand up for yourself with
that

Yeah i do

And not let them decide
what is best for your body

Absolutely! i mean i feel like
yes they know the general, of
course they have knowledge
um but they don't have my
knowledge they haven't lived
in my body

Exactly
No you've got to be the
authority on your own
experience

Exactly
And there's just this, they do
make it look like there's a
stigma, or like punishment,
like yes i made this stupid
mistake not using a – like a
decade ago, almost a decade
ago, but should i, be
depressed and lose pay once
a month and can't have sex
when i can take a pill now
and not experience any, any
of that? no, i don't think so, i
don't think it's responsible to,
to not give me the, the pills

Exactly

The pills are amazing, it's like
i don't have it at all, like i
can't describe it because
there's nothing
It's like a cure
You know?

I don't have anything

No i – no that's not what i – i
know i'm sure you don't have
anything

I'm actually uh
Totally clean

Great, i'm happy for you, it's
a nightmare

I had crabs once but that
wasn't from the industry
that was from a boyfriend

Ok
Yeah
Um
Are you
Are you getting
Like um
Like birth control or
something?

Oh no no i'm not on birth
control
Birth control fucks my
hormones

Right

No i'm getting the all clear
so i can go back into work

Oh yeah

You have to have those
every thirty days
Um
But i you know
It's not a big deal it's just a
ritual, it's just a thing
So that's, why i'm here

Yeah, so, i mean how long

has it been?

A long time
Uh
Like four years

Four years ok
No that is a long – i mean it
doesn't sound long but it is
actually i guess, because
you're not that old

No

Right
Um
God so you started . . .
I mean how long were you
Sorry is this invasive?

No not at all
Thank you for asking if it
is but it's not
I did it for about half a
year

Oh that short?

Yeah that's pretty typical
actually

Is that so

Yeah
Um
I mean it's more typical
now
It's shorter now even
At the time . . .
Well anyway it doesn't
matter i did it for half a
year
And uh
I got out
And now i'm doing it
again

Ok
Just 'cause, 'cause you were
doing something, like what
have you done in the last
four years?

It's been a rough time to be
honest
It's been a rough time
And last night actually my
The place i'm staying
Something – i just, it was
just
Anyway it was a kick up
the arse to do something to
Change my situation
Because it was
I didn't get much sleep

I'm sorry to hear that

Oh it's fine, i mean
This'll get me
This'll be good
It was just upsetting
Like a
Potential future
So i'm
This'll be good though

So are you
Um
So you say you 'got out'?

Like, you didn't want to 'be in'?

Um
It's not that i didn't
Well
Well maybe
Uh
I didn't at the time
I had a great time in the
industry though and i'm
going to have a great time
again

Right i'm sure

Yeah

Um
So you're in a bind?

Yeah, but, just a bit

So

Is this, this is a, this is a way
out of whatever you're in
now?

                          Yeah

So you're just going to go
back
Are you afraid of going back
because that was also –
No, you said you had a good
time

                          I had a great time

Yeah, sorry
I heard that yeah
Can you not get a job because
of your, history?

                          Oh uh
                          No

I just, have you considered
doing something else?

                          I get paid about a grand a
                          day
                          To do what i do
                          So
                          No

Gotcha
Yeah no that is uh . . .
That'll sort you out quickly
actually
How many days do you
work?

                          A couple days a week

That is, no, that is more than
Do you think you'll just go
for another six months?

                          Uh i don't know that
                          entirely depends

Yeah of course

I keep thinking they're going

to call my name but it's not,
it's not my name

Yeah same

Um
Can i just ask you
I really hope this isn't rude, i
really don't want to be rude
I'm just thinking
That you have other options
and they're not going to pay
a grand a day
But
There are other things
And i
I just would feel irresponsible
if i didn't
Say that, to you

Um so when you say other
options you mean other
jobs?

That i'm not qualified for

Yes

I mean i have no idea, what
you're qualified for

No you don't

No i don't i'm sorry i don't

But i do know
That, you know
Other people
But there are other people
who've made other choices
and, it's worked out really
well for them, as far as i
understand
Like i've seen some
documentaries, and, you
know it's, with some people

to help in the first instance at
least, people do really have /
a good life . . .

Yes
Absolutely
A support network
Is important
And you don't know what
mine is like
You don't know if i have
that
You're sort of taunting me,
with those other people

I just get the vibe that you
were not into it / when you
did it –
No, from
From now
I don't want you to go back,
to that, if
And i've said it and i just
believe, generally, that, if you
have an opportunity to say
something that you believe in
then you should say it and
this is what i believe
And i've said it
So i've done my job

From watching me?

Good for you i'm really
happy

I just don't want you to make
a bad choice and fall off, the
wagon

What wagon? where's this
– sorry what is this wagon

I'm just, if you need advice or
/ support i can

I'll take input from
someone who hasn't got
off to me thanks

I
If i can help in any way, i
don't know how i can help /
but i want to

    You cannot help
    The –
    And you don't want to
    help

I absolutely want to help /

    No you don't you want to
    say out loud that you have
    helped, that's your whole
    philosophy that's your
    whole mode here

That is not that is not true

    Ok great can i stay with
    you then? can i crash on
    your sofa? just while i get
    on my feet? just a while?
    just a month or so?

(*caught out*)

    I have met you before
    Not like what we were, like
    earlier
    I have met *you*
    The yous of of this planet
    I have met them
    My whole life
    And i have taken them at
    their word and nothing
    has changed
    Nothing has changed
    Ok?
    I am not going *back*
    This is not a thing i *was*
    Everything is the same
    and i took four years out
    of it like i was in a coma
    like i was in a horrible,
    spiralling coma

And now i'm here
And you can call here
whatever you like
Rock bottom or whatever
but the fact is it's where i
am
And this is the ladder
And if you think i have
other options
You are
Naïve
Stupid
Ignorant
Arrogant
Or all of them
And
And
You've heard this, we met
two minutes ago
I am living this
This is something that i
This is something that i
can
For money
So that's what i'm going to
do
And you know what i'm
not making a 'bad choice'
because i'm not making a
choice at all
All those other people who
made those other choices,
did they have the money
to make those choices? did
they have the support to
make those choices? did
they have the family? and
the friends to make those
choices?
Did they have the right
body type or right sex or
the right whatever? the

right skin colour?
You know, what helped
them make those choices,
because it's not just the
choice
It's never just the choice
I mean if you think choice
is
Then you're fucking
stupid
I don't know you
But you are
If that's
Choice is a fairytale
(*stands*)
I'm going to make a new
appointment
(*holds out their hand*)
Give me your phone

(*unsure but not really thinking
about it, takes their phone out of
their pocket and gives it, is
uneasy*)

(*taps something into it – this
takes as long as it takes*)
Buzz me if you want
bespoke stuff
That's where the money is
If you want to help that's
how

**LUCY
SUNNY
JODIE**

sunny   **lucy**
Fuck yes it hurt
Fuck me yes it hurt
No it fucking hurt, of course
It hurt it hurt, it was like a
sting? sort of?
Like a bee is stinging you

over and over
Like a pernicious fucking bee
is stinging you over and over
They call it a 'scratch'
Scratch doesn't cover it
doesn't begin to cover it
Yeah the sensation is the
same but it gives it a – a
quality that's not accurate,
because sure it feels like a
scratch but that scratch is like
in you
And so it's different like a
scratch can be nice like a
scratch your back or scratch
your arse like that's a relief
but this is like
Scratch
In your oesophagus
Like a scratch up in your
urethra
That's not where you want a
scratch
So yeah
Sure it was a scratch but like
that's not, that's not the word

So can i, would you mind
if i asked you, what it's
about?

What?

Alright ballerina

On your tiptoes
I'll tell ya
Well thing is
I've always relied on myself
So it's a reminder
That i'm myself
And no one else
And there's no one else but
myself
And that's it
This is it

So it was kind of like a
wedding
It was kind of like getting
married, to myself, like sex
and the city
Only it's on my body it's not a
pair of fucking shoes

I've never watched that
show

It's alright
They might have it here
Dvds though and they're all
scratched to fuckery (*raising
their voice for the benefit of
someone further away*) because
someone doesn't follow the
rules and leaves them out of
their cases

How much you pay for it?

I actually
Got it at a discount
'Cause i went to school with
the guy
And he just did it in his living
room, which i thought was
nasty fucked up but actually
when you think about it a
tattoo parlour is just a
fucking living room anyway,
like it's got a couch it just
looks all medical, and they
play music and stuff and
people walking in and out
and having conversations so,
yeah i had mine in like a
proper living room but it was
quiet at least
I didn't do anything for it!

What? what?

You're looking at / me like –
no i didn't, i didn't do
anything – i'm not a

No i'm not, i wasn't

prostitute fuck you

You don't have to 'cause you're looking at me like that	Fuck you i wasn't saying you're a / prostitute! no one's saying you're a prostitute! that is that is like slut shaming!
You're slut shaming me! but i didn't do it!	
	I'm not say – i'm not – what?
Listen i didn't do anything / i just knew him so he	No one's saying you did
Did it cheap, he did it at cost or just to cover his time or whatever	

You don't have to 'cause
you're looking at me like that

You're slut shaming me! but i
didn't do it!

Listen i didn't do anything / i
just knew him so he
Did it cheap, he did it at cost
or just to cover his time or
whatever
So yeah that's how i got it
cheap
But you know what i would
have paid the whole price if i
had to, if i had to
'Cause i had been saving up,
and this was, you know, this is
important to me, it's always
been important to me
(*to jodie*) Little mouse might
get one won't ya
We been talking about it
Just need to leap yeah
Maybe i'll push ya!
Nah the time will come
Something will – something
will happen and you'll be
spurred

That's private

No offence it's just private
(*to jodie*) Isn't it

No problem

Fuck you i wasn't saying
you're a / prostitute! no
one's saying you're a
prostitute! that is that is
like slut shaming!

I'm not say – i'm not –
what?

No one's saying you did

(*to jodie*) What are you
thinking / of getting?

Oh / ok i just

Ok

No problem

No
So
Do you have others?

No, no, this is my only one
I mean maybe i'll get more
If i'll get – if i get in the
position where i can have
more i'll definitely get more
'Cause i figure you know
that's an investment
It's not an investment that'll
earn you, money or anything
But it's something that can
never be taken away from
you
It's a piece of art, like these
people are artists
They're fucking, artisans
Like but with skin
And i have a piece of art
And that can't be taken away
Unless you hack my fucking
arm off
But otherwise
This is mine
'Til i'm dead
No one can steal this from
me
I can't sell it
I can't get in a really bad spot
and be like hey you know
maybe i should get rid of that
thing
Not that i would, but i
couldn't is what i'm saying
I can't do that
And that's, and it's beautiful,
isn't it beautiful, it is
beautiful, it's beautiful
And
You know . . .
I deserve beautiful things

I deserve beautiful things
I don't have any other
beautiful things
I'm not a beautiful, myself –
I'm alright looking
Like i think i'm fine looking
I'll do
But i'm not, and this is,
beautiful
So
And now it is me
So now i'm beautiful
And you know i can . . .
Whatever it's beautiful
And i deserve it

          Fuck yes

I'm entitled to beauty

          Fuck yes

Fuck yeah
So i'll never regret it
And there's nothing else i can
say that about that's for shit
sure
So yeah
So yeah it hurt though

SUNNY
PIP
LUCY
JODIE

sunny (*avoiding pip's touch*)	**pip** (*trying to calm sunny down*)
No /	Ok
No no no	Ok
No come on	**lucy**
You know me	What's going – what is it?
You know me	
We know each other	What's happening?
Come on	
How long have i been coming here /	**pip**
How long – i've been coming	Why don't we just

here such a long
No
No
I've been here
That's my room /
It's my room
I just need to go back to my
room, come on /
Come on
Come on it was only
Come on
Please
Please /
Please no listen
No but just listen
Listen just if you just
Just listen for a second just for a
second
Just for a second can i
just say something
Can i just say something
Please
I
Fucked up
I fucked up but it didn't feel like
fucking up, it felt good
I felt so good, i needed to feel
good do you
[*understand*]
Do you get it / do you fucking
get it
That's all
That's all it was
Nothing shady /
Come on you can't
You understand you
understand
You've got to
understand
Please, let me go
Please
No just no come on come on

Come on let's

Sunny

Sunny you know i

lucy
(*to pip*) What do you want?
(*to jodie*) What's happening

pip
I understand

I know it wasn't i know but
sunny we have to go let's
go now, please let's

lucy
What did she do?
pip
(*moving towards sunny to*

(*resisting pip, lashing out*) No fuck
you fuck you! get off me!
Fuck you get off me!
I need – i'm going! i'm going to
my room!
This is a fucking stupid
It's a stupid rule!
This is crazy this is
motherfucking crazy
Come on /
It was one fucking night!
It wasn't even the whole night
They left they left
They left – i had them leave
didn't i!
No one saw them!
How did – (*to lucy*) Did you tell
her! /
(*to jodie*) Did you tell her! /
I didn't –
Did you tell her!
Everything was
fine /
I didn't
It wasn't
I wasn't paid
They didn't we didn't do drugs
we didn't drink we just
We just
Held each other
And touched each other, we just
touched each other
I just needed
The touch
That's all i needed
Ok and i won't do it again / and
oh my god i won't do it again i
won't i would never i'll never
do it again
I'll never do it again if that's
what you want

lead her) Let's talk about this
outside Let's go outside, i'll
come with you
i'm going too, it's alright
it's just outside
Don't please don't do that
lucy
Don't touch her!

pip
Sunny i know you're upset

lucy
I didn't i didn't i promise
jodie (*shakes her head*)

lucy
Is she getting – for that? is
she getting kicked out?

(*to pip*)
She won't do it again!
what's wrong with you!
jodie
(*again holds lucy back,
silently discourages her from
saying anything*)

Just let me stay and i won't i'll
never do it again

pip
You shouldn't have done it
in the first place
You know
You've been here
You have been here
Haven't you
A long time
You should know
You do know

I just
I do know but i you know the
rules are fucking

They're there for your
protection

This is protection!
This is long term you know, this
is this is protection
From
From
From not being
Ok?

It's just we can't / have . . .

I get it i get that but i thought
you know i thought if i was
straight with you, / if i was
honest, when you asked me   But when you
I'm not lying am i i'm being
straight with you

When you broke the rules
hoping we wouldn't /
Pip   know that is a form of
Come on   lying
Pip!

I'm sorry i'm really sorry

This really
This is really happening

(*nods*)

Fucking fuck!

Fuck!
No! fucking fuck off! fuck
you! Don't touch me! fuck!
Fuck
Oh fuck
Where am i gonna

> There are other places
> But you can't
> I'm sorry

(*makes a run for it*)	
lucy	(*physically stops sunny*)
(*instinctively/defensively*	Alright alright – no sunny!
moves closer to jodie, who holds her)	stop this!
Let her go! just let her go it's	We can't do this! you know
her room! give her another why	what happens if – do you
can't you just give her another	want me – (*to lucy*) lucy
chance!	i'll speak to you separately
	– (*still struggling with sunny*)
	sunny please stop! stop!
sunny (*stops*)	
	(*has ended up in a weird
	embrace which they hold for a
	moment*)
(*long exhale*)	
(*held breath*)	Ok
(*inhale*)	

JODIE
KIT

kit	**jodie**
Oh god	
I am so – before you say	
anything i am so sorry i left	
you, in the, lurch i just, i	
don't know what i, but i am	
so sorry i really am i	
Is that, is that why you're,	
back?	

I
I
I
I, i do want
To say something

Ok

I want to tell you
You want to know
I understand
I'll tell you

Tell me what

Why

I was a drug addict
I am a drug addict
I broke out / of rehab and
now i'm on the streets

I don't

I broke out of jail and now
i'm here /

I

I served my time in prison
but i can't get a job
because no one will hire an
ex con with scars
I did my time even though
i was wrongly convicted,
but no one believes me
and i can't prove it
And now it's too late
I'm on parole
I was convicted, then
acquitted, and i still can't
get a job
I didn't even go to prison
but everyone thinks i did it
anyway
I did it but it was an
accident
I did it but i don't regret it
My parents threw me out
My family threw me out
when i was fourteen

My father fucked me and my
mother threw me out when she
discovered it
I ran away from home
I was fostered all my life
My parents were homeless
I never had a family, i'm
an orphan
I'm a veteran
I'm gay
I'm bisexual
I'm transgender
I'm straight as they come
and can't find anyone to
love me
I'm diabetic
I was a high-powered
banker and lost everything
in the economic downturn
I was made redundant
I'm disabled but the
government has declared
me fit to work
I'm workshy
I have children
I have children i had to
give up
I have children who
persuaded me to give
them the house in advance
so they wouldn't pay
inheritance tax when i
died and they changed the
locks while i was out
shopping
There are squatters in my
home and it's all i have
and i've got nowhere else
to go
My mortgage was too big, i
couldn't pay it
It was too dangerous there

I couldn't stay
I fled domestic violence
I left
I self harmed
I drank
I'm an alcoholic
I'm mentally ill
I'm autistic
I'm schizophrenic
I'm psychotic
I'm delusional
I'm tripping right now
I'm on medication
I'm not taking my
medication
I've taken too much
medication, i've overdosed
I want to die
I want to be warm
I want to be outside
I have a house, and a
family, and a job, i just do
this for some extra cash
I'm scamming you
I have a car
I live in my car
I'm an immigrant
I'm in a gang
I'm a sex slave for my
boyfriend's gang
I'm a sex worker
I'm hiv positive
I was sold to someone and
i've escaped
I'm lost
I'm trying to get home
I'm trying to get back to
my country
I'm trying to get into a
hostel
I'm trying to get
somewhere warm

I'm trying to get some
sleep
I'm trying to be safe
I'm trying to be clean
I'm trying to change
I'm trying to be good
I'm trying
I'm really trying

It would be a real
Privilege
To give you
That tattoo
I'd really like to
If you like it
If
You'll accept it

(*nods*)

Good
Ok
I've
Drawn it
(*after not getting the response
they expected, they produce the
drawing*)

(*looks at the drawing*)
(*sniffs*)

Is it
What you thought?

(*nods*)

Great
Great
Do you want to
We can do it
Now?

(*nods*)

Great
(*gestures for jodie to follow*)

(starts preparing)

(is led by kit's gesture)

I know all those people

SUNNY
JESSE

sunny   **jesse**
Back when i still went to
church
I saw her out the corner of
my eye
Because she wouldn't keep
still
She was just all over the place
all of the time
And i was upset at her
'Cause, at the time
Anyway
The, offering was coming
round
And everyone was putting
their stuff in you know and i
put something in
And it wasn't much but it was
ok, like i didn't feel bad about
it
And this little kid
Didn't have anything
obviously
And her mum didn't give her
anything – like give the kid
something to give to put in
the basket you know
Anyway
She didn't have anything
And i saw her bring the
basket up to her face and her
cheeks are coming out
further than her nose 'cause
she's still that chubby-young
you know

And she just closes her eyes
And kisses the basket
And, that made me think
That's always stuck with me,
you know stuck with me right
here (*their chest*)
She didn't have anything
But she gave what she had
And it's not going to do
anything
Of course that's not going to
do anything
But she gave it anyway
And i have nothing
And i don't have a thing
Not anything i can afford to
give
I
But i can do this
And i am clean
I used to do drugs but i don't
anymore, i have tattoos but
that was ages ago now
I've done research
I've got an iphone which is
fucking controversial or some
shit but it's my life it's my
whole life, you save for
anything it's going to be an
iphone – i apply for jobs and
read books and email my
advocates and do all the stuff
i'm meant to do to be a good
little hobo and i research
stuff like this
And i'm, not had hepatitis,
and i'm not sick, and i'm not
an alcoholic like some of
them are, i'm not
And this is something that i
can give
And i haven't got anyone

Obviously i've not got anyone
Otherwise i wouldn't be in
this situation
You know?
I've got no one to hold on to
them for
And i don't drink
And maybe something, some
disaster will happen in my
future to me and i'll
But you can't live your life
thinking
Yeah it's going to fuck up
soon
'Cause of course it will
Anything could happen
So i want to give them away
One of them
I want to give it away
Help someone
'Cause people have helped
me
Even when it feels like they're
not that's the thing i've
learned
That's what
A lot of people have helped
me
And i want to help, like, one,
person
But i can *really* help them,
you know
I don't have to talk about it
I can just know that i've done
it
And that's enough
And they don't even, know it
was from a, homeless
You don't need to tell them
that
I'm
You know

I'm begging you
I am begging you
To take it from me
And i don't beg often i don't
even beg for myself, i don't
do that
Creeps people out
But if you say yes
Let me do this
Believe me
You're not just helping that
person
You're helping me

I think that's all fine

You do?

Yes
I'm only the first person
you're going to talk to
We have a large team
And there'll be a few
evaluations but we can get
that started?

Yeah yeah let's get started
yeah

But just to be clear
This is the initial yes
It's not the final yes

So
Who decides?

The team decides, we
decide as a team

Ok but you think it's a good
idea

I think it's fine
I think if you want to do it
I think there are greater
risks, associated with your
situation
But if you are aware of
those
It's not our place
But i'm not the only one

who decides

I get you
You got a boss

I do have a boss yeah
But i can certainly start the
process

Ok yeah get me talking to
your boss

You will eventually talk to
my boss yes

Ok so how do we start

(*getting her papers*) Well i
have papers for you, if you
can fill those out
And i'll need a proof of
identity
And a contact for you, do
you have an address?

Not right now, no

That's ok, as long as i can
get in touch with you

I have a phone

Exactly that will do
So we'll put that on the
form
And eventually we'll need
some way of sending you
things, but we can arrange
that, we've done that
before
Um
And do you know your
blood type?

No

We'll find that out, that's
fine
(*gives her the papers*)

If you need any help with
any of these

Just ask

I like your tattoo

Thanks
I like yours

Thank you

I didn't think people like you
could have tattoos

Because of my job?
Oh no the workplace is
becoming much more
relaxed
It's not so stigmatised as it
once was
Yeah no i'm um i'm
showing it off
It's very recent
It's only just sort of gone
down
I got it whilst i was
travelling, i went travelling
recently
I did this
Um
Campaign
Uh it was a lot of hiking,
and building buildings for,
disadvantaged people in
south america
And i got this – it's a sun
An aztec sun
And the aztecs believed
that the world had been
made four times
Made and destroyed, four
times
And this is time number
five
And that's why it's got

these five, these rays
Because we're in the fifth,
new, version
Which is what it was going
to feel like
Going there
Making it, new
So that's what that means
to me

Ah was it a disappointment
then?

What?
No it, it was great

Sorry yeah no you just said
was – uh it *was going* to be

Oh no was
Was
No it was brilliant, i had a
great time
I did
I went and everything
I did
It was great

Ok
Yeah it sounds
So you're a saint then
I mean you work in organ
donation and you fuck off to
south america – excuse me
You go off to south america
and help people

I'm not a saint
No one's a saint

That's true

Anyway i like yours

Yeah me too
Like having something
permanent
Can't wash it off

This is like that
We can't put it back in

I know that
Like i know that

I know you do, but a lot of
people
Sort of
Remember halfway
through the process

No it takes about half a
year
To sort everything
So if you need time to /
think about it
Ok

The operation?

No

Things will be different
When i
Give it

There'll certainly be a
change in lifestyle
Depending on your,
lifestyle now

Ok

Is that what / you meant?

Yeah but also
No yeah
That's what
Just
Things will change

Definitely
Significantly

That's good
I want to change

The Swell

for Mom

Writer's Note

I found it so difficult to write this. Not the play – which has been in my brain for sixteen years, and poured out of me over a single week in 2018 – but the writer's note. It's so difficult to talk about this play without spoiling it in some way; either by steering your impressions of the characters, or giving away the ending, or diminishing the room it holds for multiple responses and reactions, all of which are valid. So instead, I thought I'd take this chance to list all the things that are in the play that you might not otherwise know were there:

The film my friend told me would be the saddest thing I would ever see – as I watched the film, I thought I saw a devastating end coming, but that ending didn't happen. I was disappointed, but I had an idea for a new play.
My short play for LOST Theatre's 5 Min Fest in 2012, directed by Amanda Castro.
The generosity of the actors in the 2017 HighTide First Commissions workshop.
The gentleness and tenacity of Hannah Hauer-King and Jonathan Kinnersley.
Jess and Shuna's un-pierced ears.
The diaries of Anaïs Nin.
The song 'You and Me on the Rock' by Brandi Carlisle.
Oliver Sacks' book *The Man Who Mistook His Wife for a Hat*.
The Harvard study that's referenced in the play.
Every true crime documentary I've seen about spies and kidnapping and men with secret families.
YouTube videos of people after their wisdom teeth are taken out.
The work of Verity Standen.
Always getting my name spelled wrong in Starbucks.
People who complain about historical figures being played by actors who don't look like them.
Returning to the town I grew up in and finding that all the shops had changed.
Geoffrey, who told me his heart was swelling.
My exes, who were quick to apologise but couldn't change.
Sarah Kosar's radical beautiful life pivot.
Another friend's decision to make it so that his sister didn't know she was cut from their inheritance for being a lesbian.
Rob and Sarah's place in Wales.
Barry's place in Box Hill.

The language that Hollie Rogers and I share, which is 80 per cent in-jokes.

Hollie's ex's sister's brain.

Everyone who ever dragged me onto a dance floor when I really didn't want to dance.

All the women I love and have loved and could love and will love.

Everyone who's known I loved them and has given me the gift of not being weird about it.

Blythe Stewart teaching me yoga.

My dad being so bad at yoga.

My brother hearing the song in everything.

My mom's career as an opera singer, then a speech and language therapist.

My mom's story of getting her ears pierced.

My grandmother's stroke.

My grandmother's subsequent prosopagnosia, meaning she no longer recognised me.

The poem I wrote about this, included on the next page.

The little lies we told my grandmother in order to calm her down when her brain could no longer stop an anxiety spiral.

My mother caring for my grandmother, and everyone else around her.

My aunt's sudden death, during the first week of rehearsals.

The final tweaks and trims with Hannah and the gorgeous cast that are happening as I write this note.

So much of writing isn't about putting words on a page. And so much of these pages I owe to others. Thanks so much, all.

The body but hides the heart
(a letter to my grandmother after her stroke)

Please
I beg you
Do not feel guilt
For forgetting the way my figure is built
For I am no tall, redheaded girl
With pale skin or dark eyes
I am only your granddaughter
This body but hides the heart inside
Which you have filled with love
And my face is for nothing but to show it
My lips but to speak it
My hands but to hold yours
My arms but to take you in them
My skin but to feel you
My ears but to hear you
My eyes but to see you
And if they are glossy and filling with tears
It is with such thanks that we've kept what's most dear
Not our meat, our bones, our organs and blood
But our love
So care not who enters
See not their stuff
If they tell you they love you
That's enough

Thanks to

Robyn Keynes, Roy Alexander-Weise and Steven Atkinson. Amanda Castro, Duncan Joyce and Dashiel Munding. Tom Littler, Taj Atwal, Syreeta Kumar, Flora Montgomery, Sophie Harkness, Jess Clark, Shuna Snow, Komal Amin, Libby Rodliffe, Blythe Stewart and Hannah Hauer-King. Stevie Hopwood and fellow Crowtherers Jennifer Claessen and Alan Ward. Vinay Patel and fellow Playdaters Sarah Kosar, David Ralf, Christopher Adams, Stephen Laughton and Poppy Corbett. Defectors Kelly Jones, Afsaneh Gray, Tom Wentworth and Robyn Addison. Plant Bangers Amalia Vitale, Roberta Zuric, Emma Waterford and Kat Bond (and Libby and Jess). Jonathan Kinnersley. Geoffrey Stuart. My family.

And they say that the truth will set you free
But then so will a lie

Ani DiFranco, 'Promised Land'

I know love is a stranger
I know that changes come
I know love is a changer

Anais Mitchell, 'Changer'

'So it's not gonna be easy. It's going to be really hard; we're
gonna have to work at this everyday, but I want to do that
because I want you. I want all of you, forever, everyday. You
and me . . . everyday.'

Nicholas Sparks, *The Notebook*

The Swell was first performed at the Orange Tree Theatre in London, on 24 June 2023 in a co-production with Damsel Productions and The Women's Prize for Playwriting. The cast was as follows:

Bel	Ruby Crepin-Glyne
Annie	Saroja-Lily Ratnavel
Flo	Jessica Clark
B	Sophie Ward
F	Shuna Snow
A	Viss Elliot Safavi

Creative Team

Director	Hannah Hauer-King
Designer	Amy Jane Cook
Lighting Designer	Elliot Griggs
Sound Designer, Composer &	
Co-Musical Director	Nicola T Chang
Co-Musical Director	Sinéad Rodger
Assistant Director	Sam Woof
Casting Consultant	Polly Jerrold
Fight & Intimacy Director	Bethan Clark
Production Manager	Stuart Burgess
Company Stage Manager	Jenny Skivens
Deputy Stage Manager	Sussan Sanii
Assistant Stage Manager	Laura Dewhirst

Characters

Bel, *20s*
Annie, *27*
Flo, *29*

Then twenty-eight years pass

B
F
A

Key

If a character's line ends with— and their next lines begins with — then
the lines run on as one without pause
/ marks a point of interruption
Interrupted lines are still spoken in their entirety
[ ] indicates speech which is not said out loud but is included to clarify
the intention of the line

> *A phone is ringing, unanswered.*

B (*calling*)   Flo. Flo. Floooooo. Flo!

F   What!

B   The phone!

F   I know.

B   Are we not going to answer it?

F   Who's going to be calling us?

B   Someone's sold our number?

F   Definitely. It'll just be a robot.

B   It's the online shopping.

F   I'm not talking about that again, Bel, it's necessary.

> *The phone stops ringing.*
>
> **F** *acknowledges this with a gesture.*

B   Flo?

F   Bel.

B   Are these my glasses?

F   Yes.

> **B** *looks at the spectacles in her hand.*
>
> **F** *sees this hesitation and takes them from her, placing them on her face for her, not impatient.*
>
> **B** *thanks her physically somehow, something small.*

F   Bad day?

B   Yeah.

F   I'll join you in the bath. Do your hair.

B   That would be really nice.

A LARGE, EXCITED GASP

> **Flo** *and* **Annie** *are embracing, joyful noises.*

Annie   It's so so good to see you.

Flo   It's so good to see you! (*To* **Bel**.) And you! It's great to meet you.

Annie   Bel, this is Flo.

Bel   I've heard so much about you.

Flo   You are exactly what I thought you would be.

Bel   Oh yeah?

Flo   No, not at all.

> *They laugh.*

Flo   You are – no, you're not anything like I imagined.

Bel   What did you imagine?

Annie   How long are you here?

Flo   Till the wedding! And then you know me, no firm anything, just thought I'd come.

Annie   No, no, Flo, not this year next year.

Flo   What?

Annie   The wedding –

Flo   'Wedding'!

Annie   – is next year, Flo.

Flo   I'm not an idiot I can read, I know it's / next year.

Annie   Oh, so you're staying that whole time?

Flo   Yes!

Annie   Aren't you – don't you / have . . .

Flo   Not with you, don't worry, I'll find a place, no this is just for as long as that takes.

Annie   Right.

Flo   I thought to myself, it was just a wake-up call that you know life is going on without me. Because I had no idea about all this, and like how did I not know this was happening. So I'm coming back, I'm done being a nomad. I'm putting down roots. (*Winking.*) At least for a bit.

Annie   I'll believe that when I see it.

Flo   You'll see it.

Bel   Is that because of the surfing? Your surfing?

Flo   Right, exactly. See she gets it.

Bel   Can I help you with your – that bag is huge.

Flo   I'm used to it, don't worry.

Bel   Well, Anais, maybe you can bring the car around so / we don't have to . . .

Flo   Ooh 'Anais'.

Annie   That's my name.

Flo   But it's so weird to hear someone say it correctly.

Annie   She's my fiancée, she ought / to know my name.

Flo   I know I know I just, I'm just excited. (*To* **Bel**.) I get like this. And the journey! And now I'm here and I just want to know all about you! Everything. Fill me in on everything.

Annie   Let's fill you in at home.

Flo   No let's fill me in at a pub or something, somewhere with food, I haven't eaten yet, like Caffe Gemini?

Annie   Gemini is a boutique jewellery shop now.

Flo   Christ.

Annie   But there's loads of places to eat, you'll see, lots of coffee shops, sandwich shops. We'll have a swift something because I've / got things to do . . .

Flo   You know everyone's always getting her name wrong.

Bel   I know, I've seen. Even at her work / still . . .

Flo   You're very impressive.

Annie (*teasing*)   Why are you so surprised!

Flo (*to* **Bel**)   She used to really kick off about it.

Bel   Oh really?

Flo   Oh yeah.

Bel   You don't any more do you.

Annie   Annie's just easier, for everyone.

Bel   She's actually always saying, aren't you, saying, 'Well the name's not the thing is it'.

Annie   No. It's the person.

Bel (*sharing a loving smile*)   Yeah.

Flo   This got very gooey very fast, let's go. So, Bel. Is 'Bel' the whole thing with you?

Bel   No, short for Belinda.

Flo   Oh, so it's like Baby Bel not Beauty and the Beast Belle?

Bel   Uh, right. Is Flo short for Florence?

Flo   No, no. Emma.

B *and* *F* *are facing each other.*

F *is not taking this seriously.*

B   So you're meant to do this to the sun. You're saying hello.

F   The sun would have to arrive first.

B   So we'll just do it to each other.

F   Hello.

B   Hello. So first you need to feel your feet. Feel yourself standing.

F   I feel my feet I feel myself standing.

B   Feel yourself rooted to the ground.

F   I am rooted to the ground.

B   And you're going to take a deep breath from inside.

F (*sarcastic*)   Where else would it come from?

B   Like it's coming from that root. It's not coming from your ribs it's deeper. It's coming from your toes.

F   My toes.

B   Your toes.

F   Are breathing.

B   Yes.

F   Ok hold on here we go.

F deeply breathes in.

F   Oh, it does actually feel – / If I . . .

B   Yeah arsehole.

F   If I just think about it coming from, hold on . . .

F breathes in again.

B   That's good.

F   That is good.

B   Just make that breath fill your whole body. And when you're ready you're going to relax your knees so that / everything is relaxed . . .

F   Bend my knees?

B   Yep so your knees are relaxed and flexible. And what we do is when we take a breath we dip a little and –

F dips too much, almost squats.

B   – with the arms we lift them above our head and inhale.

F struggles with this.

B   Flo, you should really be able to do that.

F   I'm doing it!

B   And when you exhale bring your hands to your heart.

They both do so.

B (*physically correcting her*)   So your heart is here, between your sternum, just a little bit higher.

F   So on top of my tits.

B   And then breathe out in ocean breath.

They do this together.

B   And then you bring them up again above your head . . .

> **B** *has only lifted her right arm fully up.*

F   Arm.

> **B** *brings her left arm up.*

B   Thank you. And your fingers are up, they're out to the world, stretch stretch stretch stretch, and on your exhale you drop to the ground, you don't have to touch the ground, your knees are still really bent.

> **F** *moans.*

B   See you're so tight, remember to feel your feet.

F   I'm feeling my feet I'm feeling everything.

B   Ok and now the next part this might be a little complicated, we'll do a few things at once.

F   Tell me quick I can't hold this.

B   You're going to breathe in halfway.

F   What?

B   So you're going to breathe in and come halfway up to a table, / and you want to make it as flat as possible.

F   This is unnatural this is, is this really necessary?

B   It's not hurting you.

F   Yes it is.

B   You're not even doing it.

> **F** *stands.*

B   Get back down there!

> **F** *does.*

B   Just relax into it.

> **F** *bounces, trying to loosen up – it's ridiculous.*

B   That's it, more like that.

> **F** *bounces more.*
>
> **B** *pauses to stifle a laugh.*

F   Don't laugh – are you taking the piss!

B   Only a little.

F (*standing*)   God you are, you're taking the piss! Look I don't *feel* stiff ok, I felt fine until all this.

B   I can see that you're stiff!

F   Well, I'm fine stiff! I'm happy stiff!

B   This is important because it will help, / it will help with everything –

    F *is breathing ocean breath loudly at* **B**, *mocking, silencing her.*

B   – That's really very good ocean breath, Flo, well done.

F   Thank you.

B   It's bound to help with surfing.

F   Oh yes *surfing, my surfing* . . .

B   Well, won't it?

Beat.

F   It's more like boogie boarding at this point.

B   Look this is what we're going to do.

F   I'm looking.

B (*demonstrating*)   You go into a plank.

F   No.

B (*demonstrating*)   Then you go into cobra

F   I see. Hold on.

    F *lies on the floor on her stomach with her torso stretched up.*

B (*joining her in position*)   Your belly has to be off the floor.

F   Fuck off.

B (*demonstrating cat pose*)   Ok let's do this instead . . .

F   Can we just stay here for a bit.

B   You'll like this.

B *demonstrates, breathing in and out as she arches*
her spine up and down.

F   Hold on, just leave me here.

B   It's easy, watch me.

> **B** *continues to demonstrate.*
>
> **F** *watches with a smile.*

F   One more time?

> **B** *arches one way . . .*

F   You are . . .

> *. . . then the other.*

F   . . . gorgeous, you know that? You are beautiful.

B   You are not taking this seriously.

F   I am very serious. You are seriously beautiful. Show me again, hold on . . .

> **F** *lies on her back, positions herself underneath* **B**'*s face.*

F   Maybe I'll understand it better from this angle.

B   You arse. You arse arse arse.

> *They kiss.*

B   I'm only doing this for you.

F (*insinuating*)   Let me repay you.

B   You know, if you don't stretch, soon you'll stop being able to make good on those offers.

F   But not yet.

HARD LAUGHTER, CATCHING BREATH

Flo   We were all getting them done, there was a whole group of us, it was someone's older sister – whose sister was it?

Annie   I don't know.

Flo   She was doing them with a needle, like really old school, that's how / we did it.

Annie   And an apple, she'd cut up an apple for the other / side, I mean how . . .

Flo   And you bottled it, you completely bottled it –

Annie   I / just didn't . . .

Flo   – and she just never has!

Annie   But all that blood, she had blood all in her fingernails / it was so . . .

Flo   But I turned out fine.

Annie   I can't do it, nope, it just gives me the – it makes me – urgh, no. Never.

Flo   Wuss.

Annie   I don't need to do it, I don't have to do it.

Flo (*reaching over and swiping an earring from her ear*)   But you clearly want to do it because you have / all these clip on ones –

Annie (*snatching the earring back, re-fixing it to her lobe*)   Flo!

Flo   – and you'd have much more range if you just . . .

Annie   Right! I can get the same thing the same effect without butchering myself!

Flo (*mocking*)   'Butchering yourself.'

Annie   It is butchery! / It is!

Flo (*to* **Bel**)   We're just going to talk in circles, you have to stop this, you, so, your turn. Story time.

Bel   I don't really have stories, any stories.

Flo   Sure you do. How you met, tell me how you met, I still don't know that, I don't know anything because (*to* **Annie**) you are a stone.

Annie (*to* **Bel**)   Do you want to tell it?

Bel   I think we should co-tell it.

Annie   That is the worst thing, everyone hates when couples do that.

Flo   No do it do it go on be gross you've earned it you deserve it you're getting married! Go on, be gross.

Annie   Ok ok, so, I, uh, was setting up the company at the time, across the street from the coffee shop.

Flo   A coffee shop, romantic, I love it already, keep going.

Annie   And Bel worked at the coffee shop. And I would go in there all the time.

Bel   She would be there at really odd times, like not the regular lunch and commute or anything, or at closing.

Annie   Yeah sometimes I would run over there just before they closed.

Bel   And I didn't know at the time it was because she was doing everything to start up the company.

Flo   This is your charity.

Annie   Non-profit.

Flo   She always was a goody goody.

Bel   She works so hard, she's always at work.

Annie   Most of the time she wasn't on the tills.

Bel   I would be making the drinks, and everyone does a bit of every job but I would most often be doing that because I was really fast at it. And I (*laughs*) one day this, stunning woman that comes in here all the time comes up and I happen to be on the till and she says her name.

Flo   Right, her weird name.

Annie   I say it as clearly as / possible because . . .

Flo   But don't you say Annie?

Annie   Yeah I would but, I think because she was taking my order and I wanted to impress her or something with my fancy name.

Flo   With your fucking fancy name.

Annie   Right, so I say 'Anais' and she –

Bel   And I, now I promise you, I hear 'anus'. And I think, why are you doing this? You're an arsehole, literally being an arsehole, and I was so disappointed like oh fuck ok she's not worth my time. So I was so mad I think that this person I had a massive crush on was being this mean, that I just I write 'ANUS' on the cup, like I call her bluff, which I absolutely should not have done even if someone did say anus, but I did. And then when her order is made she picks up the cup.

Annie   I pick up the cup and I see 'ANUS'.

Bel   She sees I've written 'ANUS' and she just starts laughing in a way which makes clear she wasn't, this wasn't what she was expecting to happen, it's not a prank, and I realise I've really fucked up I've really made a mistake.

Annie This happens all the time but I've never had 'ANUS', I've had all sorts but not anus.

Bel So anyway I apologise.

Annie She apologises like twenty times, like twenty different ways.

Bel And I give her a voucher for loads of money and anyway, that is that. Basically. After that point you came in the regular amount, used your voucher, I tried to make sure I took your order, or if I was making drinks I'd make sure I'd give it to you and we'd always, smile. And then you asked me out didn't you?

Annie Yeah I did.

Flo No! That is the most shocking part of this story – you asked her out!

Annie Yeah.

Flo (*to* **Bel**) And were you out at this point?

Bel Uh, no.

Annie Not until the –

Flo Right. Incredible. So, so what, you just asked, what on a date?

Bel Not explicitly a date but it was heavily implied. To anyone with, anyone basically. So then we went on a date that wasn't a date but was definitely a date.

Flo Wow. Ok. That is, like it's not spectacular but it's pretty cute. (*To* **Bel**.) And then how long were you together before you proposed.

Annie I did that as well.

Flo You proposed! What's going on – who are you – what have you done with my friend Annie!

Annie It was about half a year.

Flo Half a year. Wow. Ok. That's fast.

Annie It doesn't feel fast, it doesn't, what's going to / happen that I don't already know, you know . . .

Bel Actually – sorry, sorry – that's a story too.

Annie   Oh no.

Bel   No it's sweet it's funny.

Flo   I am already extremely excited for this.

Annie   / It's –

Bel   Tell her.

Annie   No . . .

Bel   She said to me . . . You're really not going to [tell her]?

Annie   I said . . . (*rolling her eyes, with love*) I said. My heart is swelling.

Flo   Sorry what?

Bel   I thought she was terminally ill!

Flo is laughing and laughing.

Annie   It was heartfelt!

Bel   It was, I loved it, once you explained what you meant.

Annie   Alright, Flo, it's not / stand-up it's sincere ok.

Bel   She goes 'For you! For you!'

Flo   That is the best, gayest thing I've ever heard.

Annie can't help but laugh with them now.

Flo   'My heart is swelling.'

Bel   That's exactly what she was like! (*To* **Annie**.) She's got you perfect.

Flo   And I know it's not the only thing that was swelling either.

Bel laughs.

Annie (*half-playing*)   Flo! –

Flo   What! –

Annie   – Juvenile. –

Flo   – What, your *fiancée* doesn't turn you on?

Annie   – Why do you have to always – it was a nice moment / –

Flo   Deny it though! Deny it! Deny it!

Annie   – and you have to take it and make it . . . (*To* **Bel**.) Don't listen to this bitch.

> **Flo** *lets out a dramatic gasp.*

Flo (*still playing*)   Fanny Annie how dare you!

> **Annie***'s face drops – this is unwelcome teasing.*
>
> *An immediate shift.*
>
> *Silence.*

Flo (*making light*)   That's it, that's the line, we just found the line.

> *Small beat.*

Flo   You did call me a bitch.

> **Annie** *counts quietly to herself, breathing deeply.*

Flo (*to* **Bel**)   It was a joke that stuck. I shouldn't have said it. Mine was BTS but I worked very fucking hard to unstick that one.

Bel   BTS?

Flo   Big Tits Simmons and before you say anything no they weren't, I was just the first in our year to get them.

Bel   Yeah Flo is better.

Flo   Much better. More me.

B SINGING TO HERSELF

Bel   This is unbelievable. Look at us! What time even is it?

Annie   Yep, that's what happens.

Bel   I like Flo.

Annie   I know you do.

Bel   She's a lot of fun.

Annie   She is that, yeah.

Bel   You're different around her.

Annie   Everyone is.

Bel   You had fun.

Annie   Yeah. I did. I always have fun, she's fun.

Bel   I'm sensing a . . . a thing. This is a thing.

Annie   It's not a thing.

Bel   Yes it is.

Annie   No it's just, I know her better than you, and she's not all that all the time. And, in a way she is and that's exhausting.

Bel   Do you not like her?

Annie   I like her. She's my oldest friend. There's no thing.

Bel   Did you two have a thing?

Annie   No. No, we did not. I've just grown up and she hasn't.

Bel   Have I not grown up either?

Annie   I didn't say that. That's not what I said is it. I'm glad you like her, I'm glad you had fun with her, and she's a good friend, she's an old friend, and this isn't a, it's just we'll see her a lot. That's what she does. She sort of, takes over.

Bel   Like that ant fungus.

Annie   What?

Bel   That zombie ant fungus on the programme.

Annie   No? What?

Bel   Maybe you were working late. The fungus that invades ants and changes their brain and makes them climb to the top of a tree and when they get there the fungus grows because it's near the light. The ant body is just a puppet now; really, it's the fungus.

Annie   Well, not that dramatic, but, but she does have a habit of, just . . . I mean, she's good fun and that's it. You think you scratch the surface and you get a deeper, but there is no deeper. There's nothing else – she's all icing and no cake. And she doesn't know – I think she genuinely – I think she's basically psychopathic. She genuinely doesn't know when she is pissing people off. That she is pissing people off, you know tonight even tonight when she whirling dervishes herself around, calling me that when she knows I hate it.

Bel   But she apologised for that.

Annie   Yeah she apologises all the time, she doesn't change.

Bel   And the drink was genuinely an accident.

Annie   Sorry, why do you care so much?

Bel   I care about you! And I had a really nice time with your really nice friend and I don't quite get why you don't like her if you've been friends such a long time.

Annie   I do like her! I really like her! I just think, I just think (*frustrated sigh*) it's good she lives wherever the fuck she lives because when we see each other we have a really good time and then she leaves and that's actually perfect. Because you know, she's this, bundle of energy all the time. She's like a puppy.

Bel   So you're mad at a puppy?

Annie   Yeah no I know that it's innocent, but why does she get to be the puppy? Why does she get to wag her tail and piss all over everything and I always have to be the human being who cleans it up? Why does she get to be the puppy! Why does no one expect her to be the human being! And why can't I be the puppy!

Bel   I'd like to see puppy you.

Small beat.

Annie   I'm just really tired. I'm not used to being . . .

Bel goes to Annie and pulls her earrings off of her ears tenderly, placing them in Annie's hand.

Annie calms down as this happens, then rubs her lobes.

Bel   They look so sore.

Annie   They're fine.

Bel kisses Annie's ears, then they gently press their foreheads together.

Bel   Is it that she's staying this time? Is that stressing you out?

Annie   She's not staying. She always says that.

A SWELL OF SONG
F BREATHES RHYTHMICALLY, AS IF RUNNING

F has been exercising, perhaps running, perhaps on the beach, only a little out of breath.

A   You don't have an answerphone.

F   No.

A   I've been calling.

F   We don't have an answerphone.

A   I'm glad you're still . . . [together]

F   What are you doing here? Why are you here?

A   Looking for you. Well, for . . . You look . . .

F   I look?

A   Different.

F   Well, it's been, hasn't it.

A   This luck. I just got here and here you . . . [are] I've got a / room in a tiny B and B . . .

F   So what you, what you, just show up?

A   I just / remembered . . .

F   What do you want?

A   Yes, so, the reason I've been trying to get in touch with you – both, actually . . . I've been doing a lot of work on myself. And I just need to say some things to some people and I would like to say sorry. To both of you. But Bel especially, obviously. For the way I . . . reacted. Behaved. It was, the situation was, I should not have done that. Um. I guess I've already, this is me already doing it but I want to do it properly so if there was a good time? For that?

F   There's not really a, good time. Bel is . . . Bel doesn't want to see you.

A   She knows I'm here?

F   No, obviously.

A   She doesn't know I'm here.

F   She's not going to want to see you.

Beat.

A   Ok yeah, ok, yep. Fine. Can I . . . call? Is there a time when you'll pick up?

F I don't think that's a great idea either. No.

A What if I wrote it down. Would you give it to her.

No response from **F**.

A Sorry, this isn't . . . This is not how I planned to . . . I wanted to do it properly. Because you're right because . . . Is there a good time? Please? When you and I can just, you know sitting down or something? Or now? Are you hungry?

F Maybe another time.

A Ok. Good. I'll call you again, so we can set a time. Yeah?

Beat.

A I'm here to put things right.

Beat.

F How long are you going to be here for?

A I didn't know how long it would take, because I couldn't get through. I didn't know if you were even . . .

F How did you know we'd be here?

A I remembered the . . . her house. The place. And then I looked and she was listed.

F We're listed?

A nods.

Beat.

F (*getting out her phone*)   Give me your number.

F gives A her phone – it's a very old model.

A This takes me back.

A plugs in her number, then gives F back her phone.

F I'll call you. We'll sort a time.

A Bel doesn't –

F Don't come – and don't call the house. It's disturbing, alright? She gets disturbed.

A Alright, yeah, sorry.

F No it's ok.

A   No I'm sorry.

F   No it's fine, but just, stop doing it. And don't come to the house.
I'll call.

B *SINGING*

F *watches* **B** *for a moment.*

F   You've been in the garden.

B   I planted all the geraniums.

F   All of them?

B   And cleared out the . . . the . . . the . . . oh the . . .

F   The hut?

B   Yes.

F   All on your own?

B   Yes I / have.

F   I wish / you wouldn't do that.

B   Stop it stop it / stop it.

F   No come / on.

B   Flo Flo please.

F   The thought of you – because / what if . . .

B   Quiet! Shh! Look!

F *does.*

B   Aren't they great.

F   Ok. They are great.

B   And I didn't die.

F   And you didn't die.

B   In fact I would class this as a triumph, wouldn't you.

F   I suppose so, yes, actually.

B   I did it all. No help necessary.

F   Actually yeah well done.

B   Thank you.

F   Do you feel different?

B   No. Just achey.

> *The smallest of pauses.*

B   What about you?

F   Mm?

B   How was town?

F   Fine.

B   Any adventures?

F   None.

> *Small beat.*

F   Coffee?

B   What time is it?

F   Well, I'm having some.

B   That's a mistake and you know it, Flo.

> *Music playing.*

> **Bel** *bops along while* **Flo** *physically drags* **Annie** *to dance.*

Annie   / It's not that I don't want – I'm really exhausted – I – I have been –

Flo   Come on you'll feel better, you'll see, it'll energise you it's the opposite, believe me – come on I just want you to have fun, / have fun with us, look we're having fun, just let your hair down – come on, for me, for me, just one – look at Bel! –

Annie   I am having fun, I am having fun, I am having – people have fun in different ways – my hair is down, my hair is literally down.

Flo   – Isn't Bel sexy. Doesn't your sexy fiancée make you want to move your body. Doesn't she.

Annie   That is not fair. How can I disagree with that.

Flo   Exactly the point. (*Half to* **Bel**.) I know what I'm doing.

> **Bel** *is encouraging* **Annie** *to dance.*

> **Annie** *submits and dances up to* **Bel**.

Flo   Yes! Yes yes yes yes yes! This has to be your wedding dance song! Wouldn't that be amazing!

> **Flo** *sings along with the song.*

Flo   Sing! Sing!

Annie   I can't / sing . . .

Bel   You can!

Flo   Sing anyway!

Bel   Everyone can sing.

Flo (*to* **Bel**)   You can sing though, I've heard you are a *singer*! You sing!

Bel   Oh no, everyone's going to . . .

Flo   What everyone? It's dead, it's a crypt. It needs your voice!

> *After a beat of reluctance,* **Bel** *sings.*

Flo   Beautiful! Beautiful! God you're beautiful, we're all so beautiful, look at us. And you know what who cares if it's Not Official. What, you need some het in a dress to make it legitimate? Some piece of paper at the end? It's the ceremony, the symbol, the statement. 'We're getting married whether you let us or not!' I say go all out. Go all fucking out, the cake the flowers all of it.

Annie   What have you had?

Flo   Nothing I'm just high on, just fucking life! And love! And life! Look at how alive we are! We are perfection! I'm just high on – but I do have some, some something, something . . .

> **Flo** *pats herself down, looking for whatever drug it is she has.*

> **Bel** *and* **Annie** *are now dancing holding hands or arms.*

Flo   I had something . . . Wait I'll get it.

> *She exits and* **Annie** *relaxes, almost slumps into* **Bel**,
> *her arms wrapped around her shoulders for support.*

Bel   Are you having a good time?

Annie   Yes.

Bel   Are you sure?

Annie   Yes.

They kiss.

*Though the song is fast they sink into a slow dance,
more a rocking embrace than a dance.*

Flo (*re-entering*)   I need your keys, they might be in the car.

Flo sees them.

*Neither **Bel** nor **Annie** look back at her.*

*After a brief moment **Flo** rushes to **Annie**'s back, throwing
her arms around both of them, making it a group hug.*

Annie *rolls her eyes but accepts this – it's actually quite nice.*

Bel *accepts it, but there is a secret beat between her and **Flo**
when **Flo**'s hands fall naturally onto **Bel**'s hips.*

Flo *and **Bel** hold each other's gaze while **Annie**'s eyes are closed.*

They rock together.

BEL – PANIC ATTACK BREATHING

Bel is trying to drink from a large glass of water.

Flo is watching from a distance.

Bel   I have to take it off I can't breathe I can't breathe I can't I'm
underwater / I can't breathe I can't I don't know why my lungs they're
collapsing I can't breathe . . .

Annie   You can breathe you can breathe shhh breathe in deep stop stop
talking stop talking you're alright you're alright it's just me it's just us
you're fine I'm with you, I'm with you, I'm here with you – that's better
good –

*She breathes deeply, leading **Bel**, holding her hands,
not once breaking eye contact, her face focused but relaxed.*

Annie   – there – again – . . . – good – you're breathing, you're
breathing – bend your knees – you warm?

Bel *nods.*

Annie *has already taken the glass of water, is dipping her fingers into it and smearing it on* **Bel***'s arms, all while they breathe deeply in and out together.*

Annie   There – there . . .

They breathe together like this for a very long time.

Bel *relaxes, swallows.*

Eventually:

Bel   I'll hug you in a minute but it's too tight now.

Annie *nods, understanding.*

They breathe together.

MEDITATION BREATH

Flo *and* **Annie** *are watching* **Bel***, who is asleep, her head is on* **Annie***'s lap.*

Flo   I'd give anything to sleep like that.

Annie   And me.

Flo   That peace.

Annie   She's got me on this no sugar thing.

Flo   What, none?

Annie   It has actually helped a lot.

Flo   A miracle. She's found a way to make you even more boring.

Annie (*laughing*)   I wasn't boring tonight was I!

Flo   No to be fair you were brilliant tonight.

Annie   I needed tonight.

Flo   So you admit it!

Annie   Work is just stress stress stress.

Flo   Yeah but you love it.

Annie   Less and less. / Poet.

Flo (*in unison with* **Annie**)   Poet.

Annie   I'm tired, way more than tired than – but now I'm in this
position where I have to decide all this, everything about every employee
and everyone's . . . and it sucks, but someone has to be the bad guy in
order for everyone else to be happy. And somehow that bad guy always
has to be me. But tonight, I've not seen her like that, especially out.
It's nice.

Flo   It's the Flo magic.

Beat.

She's great, well done.

Annie   She is yeah.

Flo   Not your type at all.

Annie   She is fit though isn't she.

Flo   She is yeah.

Annie   It is kind of weird being someone's first.

Flo (*humorously bragging*)   You get used to it.

Annie   Not first, fully first, but first *full* . . . if that makes sense.

Flo   You almost never make sense.

Annie   Like she was with girls but it was always . . .

Flo   Illicit.

Annie   Secret, yeah. Only kissing.

Flo   I hate that. Properly hate that. Hiding who you are.

Annie   Ooh political.

Flo   Not by choice.

Annie   Are you still shagging your way across the world then or is there
someone, a particular person anywhere?

Flo   It's like you don't know me at all.

Annie   What you wouldn't like it?

Flo   Yeah I would but I'm not looking for it, I'm going to let it come
to me.

Annie   It would be nice to see you with someone though. Long term.

Flo   Six months is long term is it?

Annie   Well, at this age . . .

Flo   'This age'! Listen to yourself, you're only twenty-six!

Annie   Twenty-seven.

Flo   I'm twenty-nine! Chill out. We'll get much older than this eventually. What did your mum say?

Annie   Oh don't, she's already booked us dress appointments, she's gone full-on.

Flo (*laughing*)   I mean I can't exactly see you up on the platform with those bulldog clips down your back.

Annie   But I feel like I should because she's accepted her, which was hard won.

Flo   Well, she's being very fucking cool now, isn't she.

Annie   Yeah

Flo   What are her folks like?

Annie   I don't know because I haven't met them.

Flo   When's that going to happen?

Annie   Never.

Flo   Never?

Annie   Yeah so –

> She checks **Bel** is definitely asleep.

Annie   – . . . She hasn't seen them in a decade.

Flo   What! No!

Annie   Yes. They – it's fucked up.

Flo   What they, because / she's –?

Annie (*nodding dramatically*)   All of that.

Flo   Oh my God.

Annie   Yeah.

Flo   So this is illicit too.

Annie   No. Or, not intentionally. If they had any contact, she would. I think she would.

Flo   They big-time religious?

Annie   She doesn't really like to talk about it but I'm guessing so. / –

Flo   Annie, you're marrying this woman and you don't –?

Annie   – From what she's said. What she did tell me was that someone saw her kissing another girl and told them and that was it. Immediately. She was fifteen, she moved out.

Flo   Big family?

Annie   No, just one sister but this is the other crazy thing – that sister, you ready for this? That sister keeps sending her money, it'll just show up in her account. But – *but* – they haven't spoken in ten years either.

Flo   What.

Annie   Yeah. So it's like proper guilt money.

Flo   Has she tried to talk to them.

Annie   Won't.

Flo   Not even / to let them know?

Annie   It got, with her parents, it got physical. / I don't know how bad –

Flo   Oh fucking Christ.

Annie   – had to drag that much out of her, but it got, I think, yeah.

Flo   Poor fucking petal.

Annie   Right at the start I would kiss her and I'd hold her face and she'd . . . (*Gestures 'no'.*) It was really sad. So no I've not met any of them. No, I lie, I've met her, an aunt I think. She lives in Manchester. Or she did, she died. We didn't go to the funeral.

A shared beat.

Annie   So I don't know if the panic attacks are just general anxiety or . . . And she's studying and she's enjoying that and I'm glad she's doing it but it's all from home and she's got nothing to leave the house for, so / she . . .

Flo   How much money does she get from this sister?

Annie   Well, we're buying a house with it. / –

Flo   Yeah she said, so loads then.

Annie   – Well, she is.

Flo   I'll be honest, it sounds like a dump.

Annie (*laughing*)   It is.

Flo   And out in the middle of nowhere? How do you say that place again?

Annie   I don't know I don't know, it's Welsh.

Flo   Fucking beautiful Welsh.

Annie   But, (*shrugging*) it's what she wants. It's her money.

Flo   And you? Is it what you want?

Beat.

Annie   I want her.

---

*SURFING BREATH – DEEP, FROM THE DIAPHRAGM,
STRONG THEN HELD THEN RELEASED*

Flo   I'll do anything to keep surfing. The crazy shit I've done to keep doing that – I've worked bars and taught gymnastics and dressed up like a cat for an office party, an office leaving party. I don't care, I'll do it. Before surfing, my life, fuck my life was a disaster. Waking up every morning and having nothing, nothing to wake up for. I'd never had anything I cared about and it was sort of normal but I still felt – I knew it wasn't normal. To feel that way. All the time. So it's not a joke when I say surfing changed my life – people say this shit about horses or whatever it is, it saves their lives and it sounds like bunk but it's true, because everything is in service of that now – I have jobs to earn money to keep surfing. I have to take care of my health, my body, to keep surfing. I have friends now. I didn't really have friends before, apart from Annie, and that was just proximity, you know? Just growing up near each other, just both being gay, you know, doesn't mean you share anything else together. She was always . . . We were just really different, but good mates but you know, different. It's amazing what that woman can do. It's cool. She used to fly off the handle a lot when we were growing up, because she had a lot of trouble with like, who she was, who she – I'm sure you know all about it. And I mean a lot, it was scary, and then one day after a particularly bad thing she says to me 'I'm going to stop doing that' and she does. She just does. Starts exercising, instead. It was weird and creepy even but it's discipline. And I didn't understand that. Until surfing. Honestly it, it changed my life. It's like the army, but for hippies. It takes me all over the world and I can go anywhere in the world where there's a swell – you need a storm to get one – and I'll see someone I know. Like how amazing is that. I'm free to do – and I'm free in the water, it sounds like a cliché but it really really is, it's like those flying dreams. Not flying, because I've done that, been up in the air, but flying in your dreams, it's different. It's really . . . you should try it.

Bel   That's how I felt in choir. The same . . . what did you call it?

Flo   Call what?

Bel   The thing that makes the wave.

Flo   Swell.

Bel   Right. That's it. In your chest, but also in your heart, you feel that. Sounds so stupid out loud.

Flo   Not stupid. Not stupid. You don't do it any more?

Bel   No. Can't. Don't like the, environment.

Flo   All the people?

Bel   Yeah basically. Which I hate because that's what I used to love about it, being part of something so much bigger than, being a small part of something big. Losing yourself in that. But when, when I, when, when everyone found out, about me, suddenly I wasn't the person – I wasn't part of them, couldn't be part of, it. But I loved, disappearing. Into other people. Dissolving in vibrations. Is that what it feels like? When you, is it called wipe out?

Flo (*joke-bragging*)   I almost never wipe out. But yeah.

Beat.

Bel   It must be terrifying. Out there on your own, water all around you.

Flo   I'm never alone. You never surf alone, unless you're a nutcase – for the record I am just the right side of nutcase. No there's always people watching out for you, there's a community, no matter if you've known them for twenty seconds or twenty years, that's what's brilliant about it, it doesn't matter, it's the same. I couldn't do it if it weren't for that, that community. (*Humour.*) I'm not very good at being alone.

Bel   I think you are. I think we both are.

Flo *is a little uncomfortable for the first time.*

Bel What particularly bad thing?

Flo I don't even remember now. Some thing with a girl. There's a gay choir in Plymouth, sort of near me, they're supposed to be really good. I've never actually been. Too, regular, commitment. You could, that would be a new way to – and I'm sure there's one near here, they're all over.

Bel Really?

Flo Oh yeah they're everywhere, very big in the scene.

Bel I don't know anything about the scene, I feel really stupid.

Flo Alright, well, I'm taking you out on the scene, I'm educating you. You need to meet the other special people. There are so many of us. You'll fall in love every day.

Bel I'd like that.

A SWELL OF SONG

Just before dawn.

F People will think we've committed some sort of crime.

B We're old. It's normal to be up this early when you're old.

F Let's stroll at least.

B It's coming – the sky, look.

F Move our bodies. Get some distance from the drunk teens and the people walking their aggressive dogs.

B Two drunk teens, one reactive dog.

F And we're not that old.

B Why can't you just pause and / take this in.

F Though I do catch myself in the mirror, stepping out of the shower, and my blood pressure spikes: 'Who the fuck is that?'

B This is why I wanted to do this. You're jumpy lately.

F I'm not 'jumpy'.

B There's a study, it's my favourite study – ok, my latest favourite study – they talked to all these different people of all these different ages, every age, and they asked them two questions. The first was, 'How much have you changed in the last five years?' And everyone said, 'Oh, I've changed so much in the last five years.' And then their second question was, 'How much do you think you will change in the next five years?' And everyone, everyone said, 'Not that much.'

They both find the irony funny.

F   God, no, no more change. I've done enough changing.

B   Do you feel, um, feel . . .

F   Yeah?

B   Uh . . .

F   Is it negative or positive?

B   Huh?

F   The word you're looking for.

B   I'm not looking, I'm . . . hesitating. Because, I do feel, um . . . guilty.

F   Guilty?

B   For changing your – well, your whole life.

F   That's not / . . .

B   It wasn't just me, my life, that changed.

F   For the better. For the better, for me. Even with all the . . . And doing the town stuff for you, for us, it's a small price. (*Reassuring, lightening.*) Look what I get for it.

B   Ok.

Beat.

B   Um. You unplugged the phone.

F   . . . I didn't think you'd notice, honestly. Sorry.

B   Why did you unplug the phone?

F   I . . . (*breath*) . . . Bel . . . I've lied to you.

F and **B** *have stopped walking.*

B   . . . Ok. I did think, something . . . Ok. Ok. Tell me.

F   I . . . I'm sorry. I . . .

F *and* **B** *are looking at each other.*

They are both readying themselves.

F   . . . didn't uh pay it. Forgot.

B (*relief*)   Oh.

F   We really have to modernise. (*Walking again.*) Direct debit, that sort of thing. We're almost Amish at this point, someone's going to be round any minute to make a documentary –

B *is craning her neck up and back, trying not to cry – she looks odd.*

F   – they'd think we were – oh oh oh oh no, no no, / oh no, no –

B   What – what? What?

F   Are you having –?

B   No no, no I'm just / –

F   Sit down.

B   I'm just trying not to – my eyes / . . .

F (*physically moving her*)   Lie down.

B   No I'm not – stop! Stop! I just had tears, I just wanted not to – I was welling up, I was trying not to cry.

F   What's the matter?

B   Nothing's the matter!

F   Why are you crying!

B   Stop being like this! I'm fine!

F   That's easy for you, for you to say! Just say! Isn't it! But I have to be on the lookout, all / the time, it's easier for you!

B   You can't keep thinking / like that . . .

F   You could have been having another stroke!

B   It's been years!

F   Yes, and everyone said you'd be dead years ago.

B   And I'm *not*.

F   It doesn't mean – it means you're *more* likely to have another.

B   I hate seeing you like this. And I know there's nothing I can do. Because I'm me, because of me. And I just think maybe, I think you are holding everything, on your own, for me, and you've done that for such a long time – for years. But maybe, now . . .

F   We're not breaking up *now*.

B (*laughing – a release*)   No.

They laugh together.

B   But you need someone else, some support. Some friends. You're always moaning that your parents are always moaning that they don't see you enough . . .

F   I see them enough.

B   Maybe you should see them more than once a year.

F   I like things the way things are. Is it that you want, more? Is that what you're really saying?

B   I have what I want. I don't want more.

They walk again.

B   I like it this early. This late. Them being the same thing, it's calming. That sky.

Beat.

B   Did we do the right thing?

Long pause.

B   Do you think we did the right thing?

F   Not right for everybody. But. Right for us.

Bel   I just think it would be fun, it would be exciting.

Annie   We'd lose all the money.

Bel   We'd lose the money we've paid but we'd save money, the money that we're *going* to pay on everything.

Annie   Yeah but we've made deposits.

Bel   Yeah but I'm not talking about the mathematics. I'm talking about you and me in love and that's it. We could just fuck off, we could do it anywhere, (*joking*) we could go to Vegas!

Annie   We can't get married in Vegas –

Bel   We can have a a . . .

Annie   You want / to go to Vegas?

Bel   I want to marry you. I don't want to marry all those other people so why do they have to be there?

Annie   But you are, you know with me you / get my mother and . . .

Bel   I know I get that I'm just saying, I just don't want to wait. I'm just finding everything . . . And what if we just said screw it and left and did it on our own somewhere beautiful, not Vegas, somewhere amazing. Just us.

Annie   Look, I know what this is.

Bel   What?

Annie   I know why you're doing this.

Beat.

Bel   What do you mean?

Annie   Bel, I know what's going on.

Silence.

Bel   You know?

Annie   Of course I do. It's obvious. And I get it. I know it's hard for you, I know you're scared, I know you're anxious about the crowd, but believe me, when you've done it, when you've looked out at everyone and done this with me you'll feel so much better. I did. It was the best thing I ever did. Not immediately, but eventually. I used to be so angry at everything and it changed me. You don't have to hide anymore, Bel. You can be who you are, you don't have to hide with me. We're not hidden. You don't have to keep doing that now. This is your new life, saying to everyone – this is me, this is the woman I love.

Bel *is very agitated.*

Annie   I'll be there. With you. By your side. We can have a safety word. Any time you feel panicky or anxious it'll / be a code word.

Bel   I don't need a code word it's not about a code word it's about all of it, all of it. It's about the family and the friends and you and . . . and . . .

Annie   Me?

Bel   The the the wedding . . .

Annie   Bel, I don't know what you're talking about, I don't know what . . .?

Bel   Ok, so, ok . . . ok . . . I . . . I'm so . . .

Annie   Come on spit it out, you're pissing me off now.

> **Bel** *can't.*

Annie   What are you trying to say? What, you don't love me?

Bel   I do love you.

Annie   Then what – then what . . . have you – has something . . . is it something I – what have I done?

Bel   No it's not no it's nothing you've it's – it's . . . It's someone else.

> *Beat.*

Annie   Someone else?

> *Beat.*

Annie   Who. Who!

> *She starts counting but doesn't get all the way to ten.*

Bel   I really didn't think, intend, for . . . for . . . I'm / so sorry.

Annie   Have you been, what – what?

Bel   I didn't want – have any intention / for this –

Annie   What do you mean intention. This is – this has – has it? Has something? Is this / just, or . . .

Bel   We never thought / . . .

Annie   'We'! We!

Bel   But it wasn't, I meant to say something / but I . . .

Annie   Who's we! Who's we! Who's we!

Bel   Flo.

> *Beat.*

Annie   Flo?

> **Annie** *is quieter now, more still, but far from calm.*

Bel   She's . . . She just, she just makes sense. More sense.

Annie   No you don't make sense you make no sense – you can't leave the house / –

Bel   Don't make that – don't . . .

Annie   – and she can't sit still for two seconds, you're not making sense. You're – you're just, new, and excited, and greedy.

Bel   I'm not good at all this stuff, this family stuff and / office parties . . .

Annie (*breathing, struggling*)   I can – you don't have to – I'll spend more time at home. I know I can be, with the job, but I can pull back / I can . . .

Bel   No that's your, you need to do that.

Annie   I'll do whatever! Whatever it is I'll – we don't have to get married at all if that's that's really what you / want we don't have to.

Bel   That's not, that's not . . .

Annie   Well, what is it! What is it then! What is it about me! About her and not me why not me!

Beat.

Annie   Because I know, I know, Bel, that you love me. I know you do. It's something I know, know past knowing, you love me. Stand there and tell me you don't love me.

Bel   I do love you.

Annie   Don't reassure me, tell me. Tell me you don't love me. Say you don't love me.

Bel *can't.*

Annie   You know I love you don't you?

Bel *nods.*

Annie   Know past knowing.

Bel *nods.*

Annie   So why are you doing this? Are you actually doing this? What, I don't make you happy? I have done – given you – and I'll do anything . . .

Bel   I'm / sorry.

Annie   Three months ago you wanted to marry / me and now you . . .

Bel   *You* wanted to get married! You and your mother was so keen to fucking shove us down the aisle.

Annie   Nobody forced you!

Bel   But there was so much pressure!

Annie   Why are you telling me now! Why didn't you – why did you have to fuck my friend to figure out / you didn't want . . .

Bel   You don't make it easy to / talk to you.

Annie   Oh no no I'm not having you blaming me for this. Was it her? Was it her coming on to you? She does that, she does that with everyone. Do you love her?

Beat.

Annie   Do you love her? Do you love her?

Small beat.

Annie   Do you love her? –

Bel *goes to* **Annie** *as she asks this but when she touches her* **Annie** *lashes out.*

Annie   Do you love her! Do you! Do you!

Bel *tries to free herself but in response* **Annie** *tightens her grip.*

Annie   You do don't you!

With this **Annie** *throws* **Bel** *against something, or to the ground.*

They both immediately halt.

Bel *is hurt.*

Annie   Are you ok?

Bel *is silent.*

Annie   Are you ok?

Bel   I'm fine.

Annie   I'm sorry.

Bel *can't respond.*

Annie   Are you ok?

Bel   Yes I'm fine.

Annie   No let me look, / you're – are you hurt?

Bel   No no I'm alright it'll be fine.

Annie   I'll get you some ice.

Bel   No don't I don't / need – ice.

Annie has already gone.

Bel rubs the place of contact.

B SINGING
THE OTHERS JOIN
A SWELL OF SONG
B REPEATING HERSELF STRANGELY – THE RYTHMN
FRAYS, DISINTEGRATES

Silence.

Annie   A clot. There was some swelling, from the, the contusion. But, it was a clot. Of blood. That . . . it got stuck. In the – they say, they said, like a marble in a hose pipe, and there are all these different sized hose pipes in the brain and this marble fit this hosepipe perfectly. And got just lodged there. And stayed. In the, FFA, the something facial area. It's the part of the brain, it's the bit of the brain that has a lot to do with a lot of stuff, so they don't know what's going to be affected, if anything, hopefully not anything, but they've talked about, you know, amnesia, not remembering, memories . . . Not being able to speak. And not being able to use bits of her body like one side. She does look different but I can't tell if that's me thinking she's going to look different so seeing it, seeing her different. She looks like, herself but not herself. But . . . maybe it's just because she's, lying that way. So. We're still finding out how bad, what damage exactly.

Flo   A clot?

Annie   A clot, yeah.

Flo   But she's so, but that's . . . an old person thing. She's young.

Annie   Apparently it can happen to anyone.

Flo   Just randomly like that?

Annie   Just randomly.

Flo   Why would she have a clot she / was so healthy.

Annie   I don't know they say it's from anything. It can be from anything, a cut or a bruise or a, a, a scrape / or –

Flo   What's a contusion?

Annie   She has a – she cut her, knocked her, head.

Flo   How?

Annie   But they say anything, anything, any kind of injury. From years ago even.

Flo   Years ago?

Annie   Not years / ago . . .

Flo   Because it would dissolve? Right?

Annie   I don't know.

Flo   You don't think . . . You don't think / –

Annie   I don't know!

> *Beat.*

Annie   It's possible.

> *Beat.*

Annie   So. That's what's happening.

Flo   She's awake?

Annie   Not right now.

Flo   She's sleeping now?

Annie   I'm not waking her up.

Flo   No don't wake her I'm not asking to wake her don't wake her, I'm just checking. She's not unconscious she's just asleep?

Annie   Yeah she's just sleeping. She was unconscious for . . . But now she's asleep.

Flo   She's been awake?

Annie   I wasn't there but yes, she'll wake up again and, and you can . . . talk. I'll leave / you to . . .

Flo   No I, I. No you can – I can leave you to . . .

Annie   Look, I'm / not going to . . .

Flo   I, look . . . Ok, this is, obviously this is so much. I did not, I'm sorry I . . . I can't be – you know she's going to need a carer. She's going to need . . .

Annie   There might be nothing.

Flo   No Annie, no, I've seen it. Strokes . . . There's this guy in Newquay . . . He can't even . . . She's going to . . . I didn't, I can't, this is, this isn't, this kind of – I can't.

Beat.

Flo   Fuck! . . . I can't do this. I can't. I'm sorry. I'm sorry for so much, and I'm sorry for this too because I can't I can't talk to I can't I've got to go. I'm going to go. And look tell her . . .

Beat.

Flo   Yeah just tell her I'm sorry. Just tell her I'm so sorry that I couldn't, that I wasn't, that I was tell her I was . . . That's not who I . . . Please. Please do that. I know you don't have to you don't have to do anything you shouldn't do anything for me, but if you could do that.

Beat.

Annie   Don't worry. Go ahead. I'll tell her exactly what you decided to do. Do you think she'll be surprised?

Flo *stares back at* **Annie***.*

F   It's wildly specific. The brain is so complex that basically anything can happen. So there's this guy, who's kept everything except he's lost verbs. So he can speak normally, he has normal conversations, but he can't access any verbs. There's someone who can only say 'tono', it might be his name I'm not sure. And then there's people who lose the ability to speak at all, speech loss of some sort is the most common outcome but Bel can speak completely fine.

A   Really.

F   Yep, completely.

A   Fantastic.

F   Yep.

A   So what is it with her then?

F   So she has a few things, what she has, it's amazing really, the brain – so one thing is that the signals come in from her eyes or her ears or whatever it is but the brain ignores half of it. So if she's looking at the clock she'll see 12-1-2-3-4-5-6, and she won't see 7-8-9-10-11.

A   What, her vision?

F   No, her vision works fine, and the connections are all there, but when the whole clock goes up to the brain, the brain responds by saying 'fuck 7 to 11'.

A   No.

F   Yeah. And when we have dinner she eats half of her plate / –

A   No.

F   – and then I just spin it round and she eats the other half. And then dressing, she can dress herself, she has good mobility, sometimes she has trouble with her left side but that's mostly because she just forgets about her left side, so she's always forgetting her socks and her shoes on that side. She doesn't comb that side of her hair. So it's mostly just about reminding her.

A   What about her memory?

F   Memory's intact.

A   What completely?

F   Absolutely.

A   That's fantastic.

F   Yeah. The main thing is, this is the main thing – she can't attach things in her head. It's not memory, it's – in the hospital she remembered everything, everyone, but she'd mix up – she kept thinking her big, huge, male nurse was her sister. She knew who her sister was, she knew where she was, and why, she wasn't confused, she just kept thinking it was her sister walking through that door. And so now, so she can ask for a glass, and I can give her a glass, and she can hold the glass in her hand, but she won't know what it is. She'll know what a glass is, and she'll be able to see the thing in her hand, what it feels like and everything else, all it's other defining . . . and she can't connect it. Until I tell her. So I'm, constantly making those connections for her, telling her what things are.

A   Still?

F   The brain does repair itself, makes new pathways, she's come on so far, but those things have persisted.

A   That's so sad.

F   It's not sad. It's just something to work around. To work with. She has strategies, lists in her head. You know they say 'good days and bad days', that's really true. And she, and it can be stressful. But. She stays in the house, she likes it there, the house is small but the land is big and she potters around. She does a lot of yoga, which has really helped, forces her to use that left side of her or she falls over. You know, she's never been good with crowds, but even coming into this little town is too – she has this – well, anyway, it's stressful. So she just stays in and I do the shopping and all the other stuff. It's a pretty simple life. And um, we're just really happy.

A (*pleased*)   Really.

F   Yes really.

A   No I'm not I'm – I'm really happy you're still together.

F   You thought we wouldn't be.

A   I didn't know. After all that . . . I'm so glad you stayed.

F   Well, it was the right thing to do. I wanted to.

A   Can I . . .

Beat.

A   What I did was inexcusable. You loved each other. I should never have, got in the way of that. Whatever my own . . . And I should definitely / not have . . .

F   Love. Present tense.

A   Of course.

Pause.

A   I was thinking, I could, help?

F   What do / you mean help?

A   I've got a bit of money now, I could come round and see you both and see if . . . And help.

F   You mean give us money?

A   Just like, see if you need anything.

F   Why would we need anything from you?

A   I just wanted to see you both and see how you were and and you're happy and it's fantastic. I'm sorry.

F   What about. For what.

A   For everything.

Beat.

A   I am. I'm not asking for your – I'm not expecting you . . . Do you accept my . . . can you accept . . . can you receive, that I'm sorry?

F   Yeah. Yes. I, I accept it.

A (*moved*)   Thank you.

F   You're welcome.

A   It's been with me this whole time. And I'd really like to do the same with Bel.

F   I really don't think. Really. No.

A   I know that / she needs . . .

F   It's not possible, sorry.

A   Please.

F   It's not fair on her, she's my priority, you aren't / –

A   I know I –

F   – we've moved on.

A   I just want her to / know . . .

F   She still hasn't forgiven you.

Small beat.

F   She doesn't want to. She can't. I'm sorry.

Pause.

Text tone – **F** *takes out her phone.*

F   Her ears must have been burning.

A doesn't respond.

F *tries to diffuse the awkwardness:*

F   How are you? I haven't asked that. Tell me how you are, what you've been up to.

A   Nothing. Nothing. The same. Same everything. It's getting . . . anyway.

Pause.

F   Is there, anyone? Any girlfriend?

A   I did have, I did have, but she . . . They just don't, um, stick around. That's happened quite a lot actually.

F   Fuck I'm sorry.

A   No it's alright. Things aren't ever the way you want them are they. It just feels like this is the compromise I'm having to make to . . . Basically I've got my life and that's, that's . . . And basically I'm never what they want. I'm exciting for a second, and then, something else is exciting.

F reaches out to comfort A with a touch,
sort of without realising she's doing it.

F pulls her hand back.

A reaches out to take her hand in hers.

After a beat they both exhale, a weird relief.

A   We should have done this a long time ago.

F   You might be right.

A   How long have we known each other?

F   Well, there's been a gap. But yeah. Most of our lives.

A   Isn't that crazy.

F   It is. Feels like longer.

A small shared laugh.

F   Do you remember meeting?

A   No.

F (*laughing a little*)   Me neither.

A   I thought you were going to say.

F   I thought you would.

They laugh.

A   And you know what . . . Yeah I'm just going to say this, I'm really glad nothing happened between us. I think that was . . . the right thing.

Beat.

F   Ok(?)

A   Yeah. I hope that's ok to say.

F   Why did – it's fine, just, why are you saying it?

A   Well, you know . . .

F   Go on.

A   We've just known each other a long time. There was a lot of time, and you – we never, and I know that must have been hard, that's all.

F   Hard?

A   For you not to . . . to do anything.

F   With you?

A   And you know, I was such a mess, I probably would have done whatever.

F   That is . . . that is . . .

A   What?

F   That is so arrogant.

A   What?

F   You are – you are incredible.

A   Come on.

F   Come on what.

A   I know, I've always known you wanted something. That's / why you –

F   Look this was a bad idea I should never – I'm going to go cancel the order – or pay, / just pay if they won't let me . . .

She rummages for her wallet.

A   No don't, come on we can be honest now, can't we. I'm saying I'm glad nothing happened, because / your friendship . . .

F   Nothing happened because I didn't want it to happen. Not because I couldn't have you because you're right you weren't exactly a challenge to get into bed were you. I didn't sleep with you because I didn't like you. (*Leaving.*) Not everyone wants to fuck you.

She leaves with her wallet.

A *relaxes, sadly.*

She sees that **F** *has left her phone.*

A *looks to where* **F** *has exited.*

A *then picks up the phone and finds what she's looking for –* **B***'s mobile number – and is extremely happy.*

She considers her action for just a moment before dialling the number and putting it to her ear.

B (*off*)   Hi, Flo, don't worry, I found it.

A   Bel?

B (*off*)   Hello? Yeah?

A   Bel, it's – how did, how did you know it was me?

B (*off*)   It came up on my phone.

A   I'm not calling from my phone.

B (*off*)   Yes you are.

At this point **F** *has re-entered.*

A   Has – I – I want to see you . . .

F *snatches the phone from* **A***, sees who's on the screen and hangs up.*

A *quakes.*

They stare at each other.

A   She thought you were me.

Silence.

A   Why did she think that?

The phone rings.

F, *torn, eventually decides the best action is to pick up,*
but she struggles to say something.

B (*off*)   Flo? Flo? Can you hear me? We cut off. I'm not hearing
anything . . . Can you hear me?

F (*instinctively moving away from* **A**)   Yeah, hi.

B (*off*)   There you are. Is everything alright? You sound weird?

F   Everything's fine I just . . . I'm coming back soon.

B (*off*)   Ok, nothing else?

F   Yeah, no, just . . . What was it you wanted me to pick up?

B (*off*)   Lemons. Oh and um, oh um, I can see it I just can't get the
name.

F   Asparagus.

B (*off*)   Asparagus, yes. The small ones.

F   Yeah I'll do that.

B (*off*)   Ok, don't hurry back, I'm fine.

F   Ok, I'll be back soon.

B (*off*)   Take your time. Love you.

F   Love you too.

B *hangs up.*

F   The stroke, she . . . she . . . the stroke really . . . The stroke mixes
things up for her. She sometimes, she . . . the stroke . . .

A   Why is she calling you Flo.

F   It's just something she does. It's just because of the stroke /.

A   No. No. She called you Flo. That wasn't a slip-up, why would she
slip up, she hasn't seen me in – you didn't correct her. She thought I was
you calling. But it was your phone. So what, so my name . . .

Long beat.

F   It's just . . . She just calls me / Flo . . .

A   What is it some, what some, game, some, fetish?

F   It's not a, no, no . . .

A   Is it . . . God. This is / –

F   It's just, she just calls me that.

A   – This is disgusting. And she likes it? She likes when you pretend to be me?

F   It's not pretend! I'm not pretending!

A   This is sick, you're both sick. / It's like you're wearing my skin.

F   I'm not sick! Neither is she! We're happy, we love each other, she loves me, she just / calls me that . . .

A   Why would she call / you that if it wasn't . . .!

F   Because she thinks –!

F stops herself, but too late.

Pause.

F   Because she thinks . . . because she . . . when she . . .

F can't complete her sentence.

Pause.

A   She thinks . . . Ok.

A understands.

Strange calm.

A   That's why you don't want me at the – don't want me showing up? She thinks you're me.

F can only shake her head

A   She does, she thinks you're me. She thinks you're me! That's what you meant, she can't attach things. So she sees you . . . You're letting her – fucking hell. Fuck.

F   Please, stop, just . . .

A   Fuck. Annie. What the fuck. She thinks you're me! You're letting her – you're telling her –! Why are you . . .?

F doesn't know what to do or say, and is barely containing herself.

A   How long has she – it's been thirty years.

F   Twenty-eight years.

A   Shut up! It's been almost thirty years, what – thirty years?! Has she, for thirty years has she –?

> **F** *can't respond, and this answers* **A***'s question.*

> **F** *deflates.*

A   Annie. Annie. What are you . . . For how long? For the whole, for –?

F   The whole time.

A   I'm going to be sick. There is so much here that is so fucked up. So wrong, so disgusting, so wrong, so . . . I am seeing her. You are going to let me see her.

F   No you are not.

A (*struggling to stop herself from shouting in a public place*)   You can't keep her! Like an animal! In a cage in a tower! Any more!

> *Beat.*

A   This is insane. How have you kept this – it's insane, Annie. It's over. It is ending now. I am ending it.

F   Yeah and then walk away like you always do, you won't be there to deal with it. What is she going to do? If you do that, she'll . . . You'll destroy everything, her whole – our whole – she's been doing so well, you can't / just –

A   You stole my identity!

F   You stole my fiancée!

A   That is fucking stupid I didn't steal anyone. You can't steal people, she left you. She left and you can't handle it. You take her here, away / from everyone –

F   She took me, this is where she wants to be.

A   – Christ, all this time. How dare you. Punish her like this.

F   That is not – I am caring for her.

A   Fuck.

F   I am taking care of her.

A   You're lying to her!

F That *is* taking care of her! She wanted to be with you. So I made that happen. And you know what you should be fucking grateful, because you're the one who fucked off, left her, *left her*, in that [state] – when she was scared and alone and you just left. Because you were too uncomfortable. Too selfish. And when she was calling out for you, I let her have that. Even though it hurt me. It really hurt me. What do you think it's been like for me? You think this is all some fantasy? Couldn't be farther from it. It's been . . . and there've been times – but I stayed, which is more than you ever did for anyone. I did what I had to do, for both of us. Even when she talked – when I had to blame her, her condition for me not being enough like you, acting like you, fucking like you, different to be around – even when I lied to her. I loved her. I love her. And she loves me.

A No. Annie. She loves me.

F She loves the person that has been caring for her for the whole second half of her life and that's me! I've done all of it and what have you done. Nothing. You've lived your life, and you come back now that *you* feel that *you* can. You have no idea what it's been like, you have no clue, you're in / no position . . .

A You are not going to guilt me! Anymore! I will not be guilted by the person who made her this way in the fucking first place!

Silence.

A Who else knows. Does anyone else know?

F No.

A Her family?

F No.

A Your family?

F No.

A They will know. Everyone will know, I'll make sure. I will do that.

F Please don't. Please don't. Please.

A Let me see her.

Bel *stirs – her movement is very limited.*

They overlap as they speak to each other:

Bel Oh. Oh my God. Oh my God oh my God.

Annie   I know it's ok you're ok.

Bel   Oh my God I'm so happy you're here I'm so happy ah so happy, thank you – ah – ah oh, wow that hurts. It hurts, I love you.

Annie   I'm sorry, I'll call a / I'll call someone.

Bel   No don't don't don't go don't call.

Annie   Ok.

Bel   I love you so much.

Annie   I love you too.

Bel   Thank – thank – thank – I didn't know if you'd say it back.

Annie   Of course I – of course.

Bel   I love love you I'm happy oh I love you oh help I love you.

They are embracing by now.

Bel   Thank God you said it thank God you're here, thank God you're here thank God. I love you.

Annie   I love you so much. I love you so much.

Bel   I love you too. I love you too. Please don't go don't leave please don't –

Annie   I'm not going to leave.

Bel   – please don't leave me please can we just stay here together.

Annie   Of course. I'm not leaving. I'm not leaving.

Bel   I love you.

Annie   I love you too.

Bel   I'm so happy to see you. I'm so happy it's you, I thought . . .

Annie   Of course I'm here. Of course I came, of course I'm here.

Bel   I love you. Such a relief, I've been so scared.

Annie   I was too. But you're ok.

Bel   You're here, I'm here, you're here.

Annie   I'm here. You're fine. You're talking, that's amazing.

Bel   We're here. I love you. Who else is here?

Annie   Just me. Just you and me it's just you and me.

Bel   I love that. I love that. Wow. Please let's keep it – please don't let her come in.

Annie   I won't.

Bel   Don't let her come in – is she mad?

Small beat.

Annie   She's not coming in.

Bel   I don't want her here, I feel too bad, I feel too bad already, she'll be so mad at me she was so upset –

Annie *is quiet as she processes this.*

Bel   – it'll be too much, please don't let her come in, please.

Annie   Ok.

Bel   Or her family. Don't let her family in. Don't let anyone in, please promise me you won't let her family – they're too much, please, please can it just be you and me. Just you and me in this room together forever and that's it that's all I want. Just you and me. I'm still so – I feel . . . weird. Weird. Things look different, feel weird. I'm scared and I'm very afraid. Please don't let them in.

Annie   I won't. I won't let them in. It's just you and me.

Bel   I love you so much, Flo.

Beat.

Annie   I love you too, Bel.

F BREATHING, SWALLOWING, SUPPRESSING

B   Hello(?)

A   Hi.

B   A visitor. Sorry, we just don't have people over, ever really. Sorry, have we met? I have this little problem, I'm not wonderful with faces.

A   Um, that's ok, we actually, we . . .

F   Bel, this . . . Ok. I . . .

B   Help me out, the name should do it.

F   This is / –

A   You don't recognise me?

B   Um. Sorry.

Beat.

B   It doesn't mean I don't [know you] – I don't recognise anyone.
Anyone. It's not you, it's me.

A *is clearly hurt by this, and takes a moment.*

B   I'm sorry. I'll know you I just can't – from just – It's really honestly
nothing / to do with . . .

A   We . . . Well we . . .

B   Oh, choir? Am I embarassing myself?

A   Choir?

B   The choir? Is that where we know each other? Sorry, if I saw you in
context, in the hall or that street I'd piece it together. It's not Sarah is it?

A   You go to choir?

B   When I can. Love it.

F   Bel, this is . . .

A (*stopping* **F**)   We haven't met.

B   Oh. Oh?

A   No.

B   We haven't?

Small beat.

B   Phew. Ok then. I just feel so rude all the time, sorry. Not that I have
to, because, Flo goes out for me, I stay here, because it's just quite tiring.

A   I can imagine. You're . . . You're . . . Sorry, just, you're so . . . You're
nothing like I imagined.

B   What did you imagine?

Beat.

A   Not . . .

B   Can I get you a drink, are you staying?

A   I don't know. Maybe. No. No I'm not. I'm going to, I think I'll just go.

B   No stay. If you want to. I was going to make a quiche. If you wanted some quiche? And Flo makes a very exciting salad. She puts fruit and nuts and, and . . . and . . . (*to* **F**) from cows.

F   Cheese.

B   And cheese and all sorts in there, sort of a mismatch of all the places she's been. Don't you. It's barely a salad.

A   I think I'll go. I just wanted to, just see, the house.

B   Oh yes. It's nice isn't it, all Flo. It was really falling apart when we got it. By the sea though, which we both love.

A   You've done a good job of it.

B   Flo's quite the handy man, not that she'd let on. With the internet and some commitment you can transform anything, can't you.

F   Yep.

B   Without her . . . Well, my life would be very different. I'd probably still just be camping in the one room that didn't leak, which was the loo, ironically. It was an obstacle course just to get through the house when we first arrived, the doors were all swollen so you couldn't close them properly and if you did you'd be trapped, had to be very careful you didn't just absentmindedly – (*to* **F**) the number of times you rescued me. You're sure we don't know each other?

A   What? No, I'm sure. I thought we had but I think I've seen pictures, or just heard about you or . . . We don't know each other. (*To* **F**.) Do we? We've not met.

F   No, I don't think so. No you haven't.

B   It's just something about the way you're . . . Something about your hands. I don't know, it's all a mess up here. Anyway thank you for dropping by, if you have to go.

A   The most social stimulation I've had in ages. Sounds pretty sad doesn't it, but it's about as much as I can handle to be honest. Even the singing, I mostly just show up and sing. Blend in to everyone else. Submerge. Like I'm alone. I like it. Are you just passing through?

A   Pretty much.

B   From where?

A   Australia.

B   My God!

A   Yeah.

B   You've come a long way.

A   I have. But yes I'll go, yes sorry to . . . I'll go. (*To* **F**.) Good seeing you again, keep in touch. (*To* **B**.) Lovely to meet you.

B   Lovely to meet you.

A   Good to um, to see . . . Just put a name to a . . . I've heard a lot about you.

F   I'll see you out / . . .

A   No I can – I can do that. I know how to do that. You stay here, I can leave all by myself. (*Sort of joking.*) I'm expert at it.

> *Small beat.*

A   Bye, Flo.

> *She exits.*

B   She was nice.

F (*hiding her emotions badly*)   Yeah.

B   What's the matter? (*Embracing her.*) Come here, tell me. Come on.

F   Nothing, I just. We don't have . . . Visitors are quite stressful, aren't they.

B   Very stressful. I mean they've always been stressful for me.

F   You did really well.

B   Thank you. It felt different I don't know why.

> *This sets* **F** *off.*

B   It's alright. Come on, there. Do you want to lie down?

F   No. I'll make the salad.

B   She was . . . She was . . .

F (*trying to remain composed*)   Was . . .?

B   What do you think she thought?

Beat.

B   Seeing me?

F   You?

B   Not everyone, understands. When they, I think, see me. Here. They see, someone, not free. They don't, understand. That I'm . . . Like you do. Not everyone would . . . like you do. Did.

F   Are you feeling . . . how are you feeling, Bel?

B   She reminded me of someone.

F   Yeah?

B   Guess.

F   Guess who?

B   Yeah.

F   I don't know, who.

B   You. A bit.

F   Really.

B   A younger you. A sort of different you. When we first met. She was very like you were, the sort of, way she held herself. I remember falling so . . . stupidly, so completely, falling for . . . The way you held yourself.

She is looking directly at **F**.

B   And I often think – I hope this doesn't hurt your feelings, I do often think about how stupid I was, actually. How stupid that was. I was stupid.

B *speaks very deliberately, very intently, with clarity.*

B   And, how lucky I am, that this, this, worked out in the end. Because if it hadn't worked out . . .

She is sending a message between her words.

B   I'd like to apologise to Anais. I should do that, somehow. I should have so long ago. I really was in love with, Anais. On this, deep . . . And,

and I really didn't know what to do with that. And so when this jolt came along and . . . Well, anyway, thank God you were, who you were. You were really what I needed. Thank you so much for being what I needed.

Perhaps **F** *understands.*

F You were what I needed too.

B I've only fallen more and more in love with you. I'll make the quiche. But we might not have everything for the base, so it'll probably be more like an omelette. But we can still call it a quiche.

F can only smile, searching **B**'s *face.*

B You know I love you.

F I love you too.

B Past knowing. (*Deliberately repeating herself.*) I love you.

Beat.

F I love you too.

B very gently pulls off **F**'s *clip-on earrings, places them in* **F**'s *palm and rubs* **F**'s *lobes.*

They gently press their foreheads together.

At the same time:

A FINAL SWELL OF SONG – SADNESS AND JOY TOGETHER AS LIGHTS DIM
